PETER Y

PETE

R YORK'S

EIGHTIES

Peter York and Charles Jennings

BBC BOOKS

ACKNOWLEDGEMENTS

I want to thank everyone in the huge and wonderful team at BBC Music & Arts who made things happen; but especially Kim Evans, Sally Angel and Charles Hunter. And the team at BBC Books who've shaped and honed and beautified this book: Heather Holden-Brown, Vanessa Daubney, Frank Phillips and Harry Green. And particular thanks to Michael Jackson, Controller of BBC2, for seeing the point immediately and running with it.

Peter York writes and broadcasts about social style, social groups and social change. He was Style Editor of *Harpers & Queen* from 1980 to 1986. He co-wrote, with Ann Barr, *The Official Sloane Ranger Handbook*, the 1980s Number One bestselling trade book, and the two Sloane Ranger books which followed. He also wrote two other books of crucial eighties social observation: *Style Wars* and *Modern Times*. His television work includes a South Bank lecture on British design – 'Punk and Pageant'.

He also has a real day job, running the management consultancy, SRU Ltd, which he co-founded twenty-one years ago. He lives in central London.

Charles Jennings was born in London and was educated there and at Oxford. He is married with two children, and lives in London where he works as a writer and journalist. His previous books include *The Confidence Trick, Now We Are Thirtysomething* and, most recently, *Up North*.

This book is published to accompany the television series entitled *Peter York's Eighties* which was first broadcast in January 1996.

The series was produced by BBC Music & Arts.

Executive Producer: Sally Angel

Series Producer: Charles Hunter

Published by BBC Books, an imprint of BBC Worldwide Publishing.

BBC Worldwide Limited, Woodlands, 80 Wood Lane, London W12 0TT

First published 1995

© Peter York and Charles Jennings 1995

The moral right of the authors has been asserted

ISBN 0 563 37191 9

Designed by Harry Green

Set in 12/18 Adobe Garamond

Printed in Great Britain by Cambus Litho Ltd, East Kilbride

Bound in Great Britain by Hunter & Foulis Ltd, Edinburgh

Colour separations by Radstock Reproductions Ltd, Midsomer Norton

Cover printed by Richard Clays Ltd, St Ives plc

CONTENTS

INTRODUCTION

My burden and delight in the early nineties, when I'd practically given up writing and broadcasting in favour of my business, was to be a soundbite/one-liner merchant for journalists and TV researchers who wanted something quick over the telephone. They often asked about the nineties. What was the spirit of the age? More importantly, what was the style of it? What trends could I see emerging? I found all these questions, which assumed as given that the eighties was in some way over and a pendulum reaction upon us, almost impossible to answer with my usual shallow facility. The fact was I couldn't see any nineties to speak of then. The cautionary tales from the eighties were all around us – the recession, the disgraced business celebrities, the 'fallen leader' – making leading eighties boosters distinctly shy about saying 'business as usual'. My answer was to say that frankly I couldn't see many positive nineties trends to speak of – the main trend was a huge default, a great lack of confident eightiesness – and I'd keep them posted.

But it drove me to talk to people, quite obsessively, about the eighties. How was it for you? What did it feel like? What emerged was that many of them were in denial, as our psychological friends say; they didn't want to think about it and they almost didn't want to admit they were there. They'd all heard about 'the greedy decade', about 'selling the family silver' and the victory of hype over substance and they tended to parrot it back at me – and the more educated, media-junkie-ish the more so. But when you pressed them to talk from their own experience a different picture emerged. Many of them were shy of owning up to how much they'd enjoyed the eighties and how much they wanted them back, for fear of sounding un-cool or non-PC. And the positive memories weren't just about getting things – hugely important as that was – but they were about the mood of it can be done in which they got them (the more 'ordinary' the people I talked to, the more readily they said that the money had been good, the opportunities had been good and the world had looked exciting). These personal experiences, moods and illusions appeared to be much more crucial to the decade than the landmark events like the Falklands War, the Royal Wedding, the Toxteth riots – every decade has landmark events.

It seemed like therapy for them – and certainly for me because I'd had a very good time – to explore those moods. Other Peters – Kellner, or Jay – could deal with the political or the economic history. Those large format picture books – the national newspapers do them very well – could deal with HMS Sheffield, the Royal Wedding balcony shots and Toxteth in flames. Capturing moods meant tracing the emergence of big themes, particular to the eighties: having money (Plutocrats); the house mania (Property); the rise of the Communication class (Pushers) and guilt-free consumer luxury (Paradise). These themes are held in place by the first chapter (Pioneers) which looks at the 1970s ideological groundwork and proselitizers and the last (Post) which looks at the eighties legacy.

One particular picture sums it all up and I nagged Harry Green, the book's designer, to get it in in multiples. It shows a certain shape of window – or door, or atrium – huge, arched, wholly glazed, with a vaguely Georgian-cum-Joseph-Paxton-Crystal-Palace pattern of glazing bars. It's absolutely everywhere, on eighties buildings at every level, from city giants like Broadgate to modest provincial business parks. And in every business-to-business commercial. And you don't need to be a Post-Modern Master of Semiotics to guess what it means.

P I O N E E R S

Pick a decade, not just any decade. Pick the 1980s – ten years of having it all. But then, the eighties are really more than a decade. The eighties are a long story about fun, greed and money. The eighties are what happened when what looked like the majority went out and took what the minority had previously thought of as its own. It was a bloodless revolution. Monopoly was no longer a game for 2-6 players. We expected something big. We expected Big Brother. We got the Big Bang. *Big* became the byword of the eighties: think, buy, dress, dream – BIG.

But even before the eighties were under way, we'd been warned that something was in the air. In the late seventies, all was grey, grim and glam-free. The Right had given up on an empire long gone; the Left clung to a utopia that would not come. Something was changing. Meanwhile, the people waited, like Dorothy in Kansas, in monochrome, not knowing that there was a world of colour somewhere over the rainbow: fed up with being Cinderellas, this time they were going to the ball....

Everyone wanted to go to the ball. *Everyone* wanted everything. And somewhere in London, the city that was once the capital of the world, two very different groups of people conspired to bring the ball to them: the Plotters and the Posers. The New Right and the New Romantics. They rose from seventies roots to set the guidelines for clubland and party politics throughout the eighties. And this is where it all begins, with the Plotters.

Days Of Darkness

The lights went out in 1974. The miners had instituted an overtime ban at the start of the winter of 1973 and, by January of the following year, the whole country was closed: three-day weeks, constant power cuts, Lord Carrington installed as Energy Secretary, followed (with consummate timing) by a full-blown miners' strike in the February. Edward Heath's modernizing government, which had entered in 1970 with a mandate to clean up the British economy, was practically dead. The British sat in the dark for a few more weeks, until the general election of 28 February, at which point Harold Wilson returned to lead a minority Labour government, the Bank of England printed more notes for the miners and the lights went back on again – a traditional British compromise. Six months later, at the start of October, Labour held another general election, edged out the Tories once more and shored up their electoral freehold with a parliamentary majority of three.

What Is To Be Done?

This did not go unnoticed at Conservative Central Office. The headline was that Heath was still in charge, at least for the time being: the subtext was that he was finished and the question was who was going to take over: Margaret Thatcher or William Whitelaw – both seen as caretaker leaders – while the party got on with the business of slugging it out for the next real prime minister. The script changed, however, on 11 February 1975 when Mrs T. *walked it*, with 146 votes to Whitelaw's 79. Julian Critchley promptly characterized it as the Peasants' Revolt.

Thatcher was still metamorphosing in those days. It wasn't just the Thatcher Look – the hair, the eyes, the power suits – which was still some way off, nor the husky, I'm-in-command contralto; her policies were in the makeover stage too, still being worked into shape. She knew what she wanted, but she wasn't entirely sure what it was called or how to get it. Fortunately, the Centre for Policy Studies and Sir Keith Joseph and Alfred Sherman were on hand to work on the problem. And as it turned out, it didn't take nearly as long to solve as the hair.

The Centre for Policy Studies (CPS), an early think-tank, was actually a product of the Heath administration. He had let it find a pitch within the party, ostensibly to do some non-threatening research into things like the differences between the European and Japanese economies but in reality to give Sir Keith Joseph something safe to do. Under his leadership, however, the CPS started to postulate all kinds of weird experiments on the British economy and British society. By 1974, the organization was acting as a greenhouse for a new Tory Party, and an entirely new philosophy was growing up in the heart of the old one. By the time Mrs Thatcher was installed, the CPS was in absolutely full flow, churning out papers and memoranda and speeches and what have you, all of them arguing massively for a shift to the Right, a shift in favour of free-market economics, monetary controls and individual liberties.

Sir Keith Joseph was the CPS front man at this stage. And yet, though he lead from the front and went out on the road and made the speeches and had the political profile, he was acting as a propagandist for the unknown Alfred Sherman, a man who made a profession of thinking the unthinkable and then trying it out on the first person he could find, to see what effect it had.

The Revolution Starts Here

Alfred Sherman was the key to several things about the New Britain in the making. First off, he wasn't a Tory at least he wasn't a born-to-rule, *noblesse oblige*, One Nation grandee, a Macmillan, a Douglas-Home, an Ian Gilmour. He was a pre-war Left-winger from Hackney who joined the International Brigade in 1937 to shoot Fascists in Spain and who returned a Marxist in 1938. After the war he went to the London School of Economics and then became a journalist, ultimately ditching socialism and winding up on the *Daily Telegraph* as a leader writer. In other words, he was a tough, clever, highly educated, highly experienced, working-class boy with an awful lot on his mind, and he was a *convert*. There was nothing automatic about his Toryism; it had involved something of a Pauline conversion to get from where he started to where he was now. Not at all the stuff of Bournemouth conferences; a thousand miles from WI

WI coffee mornings and local candidates in chalkstripes driving off to the shires. Sherman was a radical. But then, the Conservative party was just ready for that.

He was also crazy about *ideas*. Up to this point, *ideas* had always been the preserve of the Left. Tories thought pragmatically, most of the time, buying into whatever ideology seemed appropriate for the occasion. Since the war, most of them had gone along with interventionist Keynesian economics because, well, did anyone else have any better ideas? Sherman did. He had hundreds of them. But principally he argued that the post-war consensus and deficit financing were losers; and that tough monetarist policies were the only answer to Britain's failure as a nation. He was utterly uncosy.

And Keith Joseph listened, and learned, and took it all on board. A strange pairing: the assertive (some said obnoxious), hard-headed, combative Sherman; and Sir Keith, a baronet, Harrow and Magdalen College, Oxford, a fellow of All Souls, hopelessly honest and intellectually conscientious to the point of self-strangulation. What were they doing together? Well, they were both searching for the Truth and they were both clever outsiders. Sherman had come up from the bottom from the bottom, while Sir Keith had come in from the top, radiating unworldliness and a lack of political instincts, which made his colleagues despair of him. And they were both Jewish: no small matter, this, in a party which, although once led by Disraeli, was notoriously, casually, anti-semitic. When Harold Macmillan said of Keith Joseph, in 1976, that he was the 'only boring Jew I've ever met', he was speaking with the authentic voice of the Party....

So Sherman and Joseph bonded uncomfortably: and in September 1974, Sir Keith went out and delivered a speech in Preston

A latter-day Alfred Sherman —
this man changed your life.

11

INTERVIEW

SIR ALFRED SHERMAN

Former Director of Studies and Co-founder, CPS

Q What was the CPS's mission as far as you were concerned?

A As far as I was concerned it had a double mission: one was to serve Keith [Joseph] and then, increasingly, Margaret with ideas, speeches, contacts. The other was to run a very small body... to influence the climate of opinion from the top. [But] you couldn't change people's views overnight. That's why I said: 'Think the unthinkable, question the unquestioned, say the unsayable,' and if what you were saying related to people's experience – they had the feeling that things weren't quite right, the stock of ideas with which they'd entered the post-war period was past its shelf date – then it would influence the thinking not only of your supporters but also of opponents and the other parties.

Q What in particular were you tilting against with the CPS?

A The idea, first, that we knew everything, [that] the government, by pulling strings or levers, could shape society. We wanted people to understand the greater complexity of it: the role of public opinion, the role of religion, the unknowability of many economic processes – many of the truths which Adam Smith has expressed, that people worked best when they were working in their own interests. But nevertheless I tried, although they were against this, to emphasise the importance of the nation, that economics is simply one part of a much wider social process, and unless you have a healthy body politic you can't have a healthy economy. These were some of the ideas: the importance of charity, the importance of people doing things for their fellow men other than simply paying their taxes and leaving it to them. We tried to make people realize that state education had failed. People should have some control over education. And that council housing cost probably ten times per unit [more] than private housing does. They wanted people to look at what had happened with clear eyes instead of believing [it] must be for the best, because it had happened. They even questioned the Welfare State, what does 'welfare' mean? What does 'State' mean? Does it mean wellbeing or does it mean what the State gives you, and does State mean the country or the government? We tried to question everything, which again is not new.

Q Finally, the reality of the Tory achievement through to 1990 and beyond was something you found rather disappointing, wasn't it?

A Yes, well... They never solved the problem of government expenditure. And if you can't solve the problem of taxation and borrowing, and you can't solve the problem of pressure on prices, and then you try to offset that pressure by monetary squeeze that slows down the economy. The key to it was government expenditure.

where he introduced the world to the idea of monetarism. In 1975, he made a speech at Oxford, where he elaborated the idea of the social market economy (a kind of economic liberalism based on the theories of Ludwig Erhard and the Mont Pelerin society). In 1976, he delivered the Stockton Lecture and called it 'Monetarism Is Not Enough', pointing out that on the one hand, a Tory government should eschew the old laissez-faire economic free-for-all of the nineteenth century, but at the same time, should have nothing at all to do with 'the use of demand creation as a short cut to growth and full employment…'.

Mrs Thatcher, by now MC of the CPS, listened, too. And here's a thing: wasn't she just a bit like Alfred Sherman herself? Her Methodist, small-trader social background was nil in nob terms; she had no interest in propping up old-style Toryism; she

Sir Keith Joseph prophesies the next ten years, while Mrs Thatcher shuts her eyes and dreams it all in visions of radiance.

wanted a form of words, an intellectual framework for her *instincts* which would allow her to get Britain by the neck and shake some sense into it. Pretty soon, Sherman was deluging her with notes and memoranda and opportunities for dialogue, and she was boning up on Hayek and the Freedom Brigade in a most diligent way and asking for more homework. And pretty soon she was driving people like Old Tory James Prior up the wall with her constant citings of Sherman's philosophy. It became her catchphrase: 'But Alfred says… ' she said.

An Old, Cold, Defeated World

You have to try and remember where everyone else was, while all this was going on. If you look at it cold, this little cabal of Thatcher, Joseph and Sherman comes across as no more than a band of crazies plotting the downfall of the World As We Know It. But at the time, the World As We Know It was destroying itself quite satisfactorily. In fact, a little apocalyptic free-thinking fitted in just fine. Quite apart from the miners' strike, the trains were hit by an overtime ban, the ambulance drivers were on strike, industrial output had ground to a halt, inflation was *averaging* 14.5 per cent a year, growth of the GDP had almost halved and, in 1976, the International Monetary Fund (IMF) moved in to take over the economy: which *really* made us feel our Third World membership.

And there was this feeling that nothing could be done. union intransigence and government ineptitude were the order of the day, and every day for evermore. When Wilson resigned in 1976 and Callaghan took over, he saw his principal role as managing Britain's decline. We weren't just in the doldrums, we were paralyzed.

With nothing to lose, you might as well go for something radical rather than evolutionary. And the CPS did. And more people started to come on board. David Young (now Lord Young of Graffham), a self-made businessman of no previously very strong political leaning, was nonetheless so impressed by Sir Keith's speeches of 1974-5 that he volunteered his services. Alan Walters, who came to feature perhaps a little too heavily later on in the eighties, was in touch with both Sherman and Joseph. And an ex-teacher and small business woman called Teresa Gorman, who had stood as an Independent, Libertarian candidate in 1974, was turning out populist pamphlets in her own industrious way on deregulation, economic liberalism and the rights of the individual.

Even more significant were John Hoskyns and Norman Strauss, who both appeared in the CPS world in 1975. Hoskyns was a suave Wykehamist who'd made a fortune out of computer systems; Strauss was a suburban Buller Act meritocrat, who'd been at Kilburn Grammar School at the same time as Sam Brittan and had gone on to become a marketing expert with Unilever. 'It is only conflict that can ensure issues are discussed,' was the kind of thing Strauss came out with. Both saw themselves, basically, as apolitical technocrats, interested in problem-solving rather than working within the antique party systems. In August 1976, Strauss produced a CPS document called 'The Need For New Data', which gives you some idea of where he was coming from. Hoskyns was a compulsive communicator, whose favourite expression was that Britain was 'Going down the tube'. Thatcher loved them. No High Table paternalism there. Clever outsiders? *Welcome them in.*

Transfigured through faith vindicated: Teresa Gorman in 1989.

Consolidation (Beseiging The Citadel Of Tory Proprieties)

Things were warming up from 1976 to 1978. Thatcher was properly installed at the head of the party and priorities were being shaped. In the pink corner were a couple of think-documents which the party had brought out, in a somewhat collective way, in 1976 and 1977: 'The Right Approach' and 'The Right Approach To The Economy'. The latter in particular was a real compromise, an old-world fit-up, involving Sir Keith Joseph, Geoffrey Howe, David Howell and James Prior: in

INTERVIEW

TERESA GORMAN
MP

Q How did you start as a political animal?

A I ran a company, started in the seventies when VAT rules were introduced. The Labour Government at that time introduced an extra tax on the self employed, who were generally reckoned to be fiddling the system. I was desperately using all my savings and all my energy to try and get a business going. And it was that sense of resentment that the government was stealing my time, as well as taking more of my money, that politicized me.

Q Had you had political thoughts before?

A No. I was brought up as a child in the fifties when Labour and Socialism dominated society. We were made to feel very bad about making money and getting on in the world. Every time you mentioned some success you had people saying, 'It's all right for you, you're making money.' A sort of resentment of success. As a young teacher, I went to the States for a few years. It was a revelation. In America everybody wanted to make money and get on in the world, and be the President. When I came back to Britain – back into this cloying and condemnatory society – I felt that I was sinking back into the past. But then Margaret Thatcher became the

Leader of the Conservative party. It was like a revelation. She brought in a millennium of hope and liberation – that's how I saw her. And it was at that stage when I got used to the idea that politics was a useful activity and not just an obstacle.

Q So were you completely apolitical apart from VAT demos before Margaret appeared on the scene, or had you not become a Tory or done anything like that?

A I was never a member of a political party until about 1976. In 1974 I stood for Parliament as an Independent. Edward Heath was Prime Minister. We were so fed up with the Conservative Party that we decided to put up our own candidate. We drew straws, and I drew the short straw, so I became the candidate. I published a manifesto in which I called for less government, less taxes and more choice. I paid my deposit in gold Krugerands, to make the point that money was being devalued rapidly by the politicians. This got into the papers and the people in the IEA picked it up. I think they saw in me a natural soul mate – a sort of suburban primitif... They invited me to one of their lunches. I met all sorts of people; politicians, gurus and academics.

Q What do you think they made of you?

A I've no idea. They were proselytizing about their wonderful views which were going to change the world, busily converting Margaret Thatcher, Nigel Lawson and Geoffrey Howe, and the younger turks;

Peter Lilley and Michael Portillo and John Redwood. They were dealing at the academic level. But here I was, a green sprout, growing in suburbia, who apparently shared their views. In those days I was very shy and would never have spoken out in the way I do now. But I met other people like Alfred Sherman. He became the first director of the Centre for Policy Studies, which Margaret Thatcher and Keith Joseph set up when she became Leader. And Alfred got me to serve on one of his endless committees to do with small businesses – because I was very deeply into anti-regulation. I wrote some pamphlets there, which he published. One which John Redwood, who by then was working in Margaret Thatcher's think tank in Downing Street, took up and introduced to Margaret... It helped to stimulate the government's initiative on small firms and enterprise, getting rid of, regulations.

Q How did it make you feel, the eighties, when you'd been given respectability?

A I felt liberated. I felt socialism, the great incubus for all those years, was suddenly being thrown out. I loved it. I thought the country was being re-born. I felt we'd got a government which would go along with people's natural instincts.

Q So what did you think was going to happen when Mrs Thatcher was elected? What would the world look like?

A I realized there was a serious job of work to be done taking the unions in hand, taking inflation in hand. If you ran a company, you knew that your money was literally being constantly devalued. It's a nightmare to try and keep your profit margins.

Q Did the eighties deliver for you? Did you get what you wanted in terms of a new Britain? Or did it fall short?

A You're never satisfied with what you get, and I certainly don't think we've gone far enough towards removing the regulations that control people's lives – in the business world particularly.

Q And you still feel what you felt in the early seventies only more so?

A Yes I do. There's still an enormous amount to be done in politics. I want politics to continue to try to liberate people rather than trap them.

other words, covering most aspects of mid-seventies couth Toryism and as a result, offending none of them. Indeed, 'The Right Approach To The Economy', had a strong flavour of the old hedged days about it. Large-scale public spending and ownership were still a necessity in some form or other, taxation of income rather than expenditure the norm, privatization just a distant dream… .

Towards A New Jerusalem

But in the blue corner, was 'Stepping Stones', produced by the CPS – effectively John Hoskyns and Norman Strauss, in this instance – in 1977. And this was the real meat: this advocated turning the world on its head, starting with the whole trades union movement. 'A landslide is needed,' said 'Stepping Stones', 'but it must represent an explicit rejection of socialism and the Labour-trades unions axis.' What's more, 'To compete with Labour in seeking peaceful co-existence will ensure continued economic decline, masked initially by North Sea oil… There is nothing to gain… and everything to lose by such a "low risk" approach.' Throw that post-war consensus clean out of the window! It's dead! It doesn't work any more! Mrs Thatcher's eyes apparently 'lit up' when she read 'Stepping Stones' and the final lines of its summary were prophetic: 'Skilfully handled, however, the rising tide of public feeling could transform the unions from Labour's secret weapon into its major electoral liability…'.

Seditious stuff. It went round the Shadow Cabinet at the end of 1977 and into 1978 and Hoskyns and Strauss did their best to sell it to the Priors and Gilmours of this world. But they weren't having it… at least, not for the time being. Still, there was plenty to be done elsewhere. The CPS had already broken the ice with a pamphlet by Sam Brittan, called 'Second Thoughts On Full Employment' and followed that with 'History, Capitalism and Freedom', by the historian Hugh Thomas. And Sherman was still churning out messages, quite promsicuously sometimes, taking in everything from 'Britain's Ethnic Problems' in 1977, to the 'Labour Party In Wales', in 1979.

Ideas Mean Power

At the same time, the number of little think-tanks and bright-ideas departments in and around the Conservative Party was multiplying like an amoebal growth. New Right was *hot*, intellectually. The Liberal Hour was out of fashion; the sharper young, significantly enough, showed a taste for liberal-bashing in their music and humour by 1977. There were fringe actvists in the National Association for Freedom, or NAFF (far-out, Feudal Britain stuff, mainly); there was the IEA (Institute for Economic Affairs) which dated back to the sixties and which went on to spawn the SAU (Social Affairs Unit) and then collaborated with the AEI (American Enterprise Institute) on free-market visions.

And then there was the ASI, the Adam Smith Institute, founded in 1976 by three academics from St Andrews: Eamonn Butler, Stuart Butler and Madsen Pirie – the man in the bow tie – and which soon became *the* right-wing shoot-from-the-hip organization, partly funded by Sir James Goldsmith (who plugged the ASI relent-lessly in *Now!* magazine) and Sir Clive Sinclair, the popular science entrepreneur. All these little hotbeds of revolution… toiling away like creatures in the diamond mines, tapping away at the Tory party's collective consciousness… It's easy to forget now that the political/economic landscape was once entirely different, that the free market, the politicization and encouragement of individual wealth (Keith Joseph, prompted by Sherman, had said we *needed* more millionaires; *needed* more inequality), the libertar-ian line on government duties and responsibilities, the emasculation of union power, actually came *from* somewhere; that they weren't always about us, in the atmosphere. These dumb acronyms, the CPS, the ASI, the IEA, were the foundations on which the next decade were built. *This is where it came from.*

Keepers Of The Flame

Not that everyone in the Tory party was necessarily wild about this arrangement. Thatcher and Joseph and Howe may have bought into this bristling new world view, but plenty hadn't. The CRD (Conservative Research Department) didn't buy in at all. The CRD had been around a good deal longer than the CPS, and was basically a research and reference organization for the party. It was headed by an ex-Balliol soft Tory, Chris Patten a natural-born One Nation Conservative, a Heathite, ameliorist type who clearly hated the CPS and saw the battle for the party's soul as an absolute Manichean showdown. Sherman, in his turn, hated Patten. 'He is a limited man,' Sherman once wrote, 'promoted far beyond his ability.' He also claimed that Patten had coined the phrase 'Mad Monk' to describe Keith Joseph and was even 'patheti-cally jealous'. *The Times*, on the other hand, smelled the odour of sulphur that the party was giving off and noted in 1978, that Sherman was 'a particular focus of… hostility' within the party.

The two factions sat it out for a while, each certain that they had the key, each stuck with the other. And it was a curious thing, the way it had become a battle of ideas. There was a long moment of stasis, while the New Jerusalem iconoclasts under Sherman and Hoskyns, wrestled with the Keepers of The Flame under Patten, all of it completely unlike the Post-War Tory Party. Ideas meant *power*: and for once, for this very reason, ideas were becoming *sexy*.…

And Then There Was The Winter Of Discontent

A Voluntary Incomes Policy: that was a good one. A Voluntary Incomes Policy… the Labour Government tried it, of course, in 1978, in a last effort to keep the lid on the whole thing. But by the turn of the year, *The Times* was locked out, the road haulage drivers were out, the grave-diggers were out… just about anyone who worked in the public sector, wasn't working at all…

John Hoskyns, the force behind 'Stepping Stones', saw his chance. By now, he was an official Thatcher Adviser, and was pressing the whole 'Stepping Stones', anti-union ethic as hard as he could on the woman at the top. Howe and Joseph were in the ascendant and the world wanted change. Even James Callaghan knew that Old Labour was finished and so, as the next general election, 3 May 1979, ground into view, things were set for the radical new world of the True Right to break through.

Window Dressing

It didn't look like that in the manifesto, though. The strange thing about the Conservative Election manifesto for 1979, was how quiet it looked. 'A strong and responsible trade union could play a big part in our economic recovery,' it said. It talked about 'Responsible Pay Bargaining' and some sensible closed shop reforms. The only business up for privatization was the National Freight Corporation. The top rate of income tax was due to be cut 'to the European Average'. It was modest, frankly: 'We make no lavish promises,' it announced at the end. It wasn't the voice of the CPS or the ASI or the IEA; it was the voice of the Tory Party of 1970. And when the party produced its Campaign Guide for the weeks of electioneering, Keith Joseph architect of the New Philosophy, got only five mentions in 789 pages; while Jim Prior, Heathite Jim, got almost twenty plugs in total. Looking back, you wonder, what was all the fuss about? Where's the rampant individualism? Where's the promise of Boom Time and Kill The TUC? How did *this* turn into the *eighties*?

(How, for that matter, did Thatcher become Thatcher? Where was the golden-haired goddess/termagant who queened it for the next decade? Like the policies: in waiting. The hair, over the preceding twenty years, had definitely changed from the original ministry-issue dark brown, circa 1961 [in the job as Parliamentary Secretary, Ministry of Pensions & National Insurance], into a fairly radiant blondeish soufflé [handy for covering up those grey hairs, too; she was born in 1925, don't forget]. And the voice had lost some of its constituency Conservative lady Nasal Whine, somewhere between June Whitfield and Celia Johnson. But there was still some way to go on the makeover.)

Nevertheless, the Winter of Discontent tipped the balance for Hoskyns and the 'Stepping Stones' ideology. Even if the manifesto said something different, more emollient, the Hoskyns view had influenced the people who were going to shape the next few years. Up to that point, it's possible that the Tory Party, that most quintissentially pragmatic political party, might have pulled back and gone for compromise. But now the True Believers knew that they could start to get things done *their way*.

And There Was Light; But With Certain Provisos

So: 3 May 1979, the compass of the earth shifts and the Conservatives get in. And in the general sensation of waking up and looking around to see what's happening next, a new emphasis builds, gathering weight and momentum.

For the theorists in the Tory Party, this was the best of times, but also the moment when they had to see what effect all the plotting and intellectual besieging and hearts and minds warfare would have when the time came to put the instructions into practice. Sherman, in particular, spent a lot of time getting exercised over the prospect of Civil Service inertia and general temporizing when the moment actually arrived for them to set to work. Having seen Keith Joseph in action in the Heath Government between 1970 and 1974, he had concluded that Joseph's natural appetite for the Right Way had been completely smothered by Civil Service advisers, rafts of Sir Humphreys who worked like fire blankets. As far back as July 1977, Sherman had written a memo arguing for a 'Territorial Army of Advisers', all pointing in the right direction, who could be recruited well before the election and drafted straight into Whitehall the moment the campaign was won.

Thatcher herself had problems working out who was to be in the Cabinet and where everyone should sit. Keith Joseph didn't get the Treasury job (which would have fitted him perfectly in many ways), but did get the Department of Industry, which fitted him like a hair shirt. Jim Prior was still definitely in (despite John Hoskyns' urgings to have him out), as were Peter Walker, Ian Gilmour and Christopher Soames, all serious doubters of the Thatcher/Joseph experiment. Geoffrey Howe and John Biffen were there to stiffen her resolve, on the other hand, as was the reassuringly dry David Howell. But it was an assortment, and the government started off by feeling its way, rather than exploding onto the scene.

And for a long while, the new government struggled with the dilemma of how to stop printing money and cut government spending back (it was still pouring out on industrial intensive-care monsters like British Leyland and British Steel), if not to the bone, then at least make a start. For all the rhetoric from the CPS and all the other acronyms, not much seemed to be happening. It was a phoney war. Callaghan, still leader of the Opposition, sat and waited for the cracks to appear.

But they never did. It took a few years for the new ideologies to appear in action, but – to the dawning astonishment of the British people – they did. Words became events. The unclubbable madmen who had been closeted in cramped, overflowing offices and corridors in the festering think-tanks of the seventies found their ideas turning Britain upside down by… oh, about 1983. And whatever happened they always said that it was a ghastly compromise – never trust a party politician – and hadn't gone nearly far enough.

Which Brings Us To Bowie

Times were strange for everyone in those days… businessmen, politicians, boys and girls… hard times, if you wanted to do anything other than dress in polyester and listen to anyone bar Elton or Rod and The Faces. That early seventies glam thing had been huge fun in its way, but by the middle of the decade, it had run its course. By 1975, you had the Glitter Band, Mud, and the Bay City Rollers, still flogging the product, Thursday nights on *Top Of The Pops*; but you also had Yes, Emerson, Lake & Palmer,

David said, 'Men it can be done,' to all those pale and worried boys.

Genesis, King Crimson music for your big, spotty brother and his cheerless friends. Disco was a wonderful compensation – for some people – but it hadn't got its second wind and it was short on role models.

Punk was on its way, true, but not fully visible and even then, it was going to raise more questions than it answered. No, there were only two fixed points in the heavens for disturbed, aspiring urban boys and girls who wanted more than reality: Bowie and Bryan Ferry.

And Bryan

Now, Bryan was wonderful, in and out of Roxy Music. Very clever, agonizingly fastidious, he managed to give the post-modern appearance of standing outside what he did – then a new posture – while at the same time, being hyper-involved and passionate. He was ironical *and* sincere when you heard 'Virginia Plain' for the first time, you knew you were listening to the natural antagonist of Joe Cocker; you were listening to a singer whose whole approach said, I'm not *singing*, I'm *being a singer*. Similarly, *the looks,* all of them, said that this is just a phase, just a costume for now. But at the same time, it mattered enormously how you looked… .

So you got dyed feather shoulders over blue spangles, or you got the white Tux with half-tamed forelock, or you got the Anthony Price GI combination of 1975 (with matching girl back-up singers, very 'sexy'), and whatever you got, it was done beautifully. And thousands of boys and girls who were sick of the street, sick of the High Street, low life, no-life, did a Bryan and turned up at the concerts wearing the Bryan look (or the gorgeous girl accessory-to-Bryan look, as in those first wet-dream Roxy album sleeves). People went to the first concerts at the Rainbow, in Finsbury Park, and had their lives changed.

The One True Original

But then, David was different too. David was good, bad, dreadful… *beautiful.* David didn't just dress up: David *re-created himself* on a regular basis. That was the one vitiating thing about Bryan: he was art school, but he was art school clever. Sometimes, the calculation showed a little too much. It was just a bit too much of an exercise in seduction, from time to time he could have been running a long, brilliant, seamless and almost undetectable advertising campaign. Whereas Bowie didn't have to think his way through to anything. Even when he was drenched in make-up (Ziggy Stardust/Aladdin Sane territory), you could see David shining weirdly through, hollow-cheeked, alien-eyed, fragile and thin. When he made 'The Man Who Fell To Earth' bare-faced and near-neutral in 1976, he looked every bit as strange as when he had the red cockade of hair and the Ziggy disc on his forehead four years earlier.

'I could play the wild mutation as a rock'n'roll star,' confided David in 'Ziggy Stardust'. He did. he made it his business signature. Not only did he switch from satin-looned hippy to short-haired cameo squaddy (in the film version of *The Virgin Soldiers*) to extra-terrestrial waif parts I & II to Hollywood Boulevard lounge spiv (white suit, flat hair, side-parting, auburn sunspecs around the time of 'Young Americans') to pan-European, pre-holocaust fade-out ('Low'), but also he switched flickeringly between sexes, personalities and classes. His nervy Mockney drone came with a strong streak of mid-Atlantic thrown in, plus a nature's aristocrat edge: all of which made him as impossible to characterize socially as sexually. Troubled boys and girls waited for his next incarnation the way the good folk of Fashionland waited for Paris. And of course, each switch of look came with an equivalent switch of musical taste.

His credibility was always in question. The line was, Bowie's a plagiarist, a *poseur*, a *packager*. His music is *soundtrack* music, not the life-giving musical essence. Bowie's only in it for fame and manipulation. Like Bryan's ironical semi-croon, Bowie's voice was always *acting*. He said at the time, 'I've caused quite enough rumpus for someone who's not even convinced he's a good musician,' and 'I've always been a screen writer. My songs have just been practice for scripts.' There was always a certain kind of rock press journalist who loved these conceits.

But this was missing the point. People loved Bowie precisely because the music came in on a photo-finish with the look. The Bowie clones (and there were thousands of them, male and female, States-side as well as Humberside, more than for any other rock'n'roller at the time, more than for Bryan, even) loved him because they put the look on a pedestal, too. The look was a way of life: it had to be. When David had himself photographed, perched on a loo, reading a Buster Keaton biography and wearing an Artful Dodger flat cap, lank bottle-dyed hair, a boiler-suit and Day-Glo plastic jellies on his feet, 90 per cent of the world thought, *freak*; while the other 10 per cent thought, *more style options – David's made it all right*. And if that in turn meant that the music became a soundtrack, that it was the strip on the edge of the film well, that's how it was.

Drive In Saturday

People took it all seriously, *so* seriously, this stuff. They wanted to be beautiful, too, like David was beautiful; they wanted to be amusing and clever and play-actorly like Bryan: so transfixed by the surface of things that it became *deep*. And this in turn, would make them heroes in their own eyes, in someone's eyes. It would take them out of the suburbs and the council flats, it would give them a licence to be mixed-up, faddish, ambivalent, style-obsessed, art objects in their own right. Aspirational, apolitical, out of it. The seventies were such a deadening time, with their crass fashions and their crushing corporatism, that this was the only way out, a way out into the fantastic. The plainer you were, the crummier and more dismally uniform your background, the more important it was to be the opposite: startling, immaculate, as unique as you could be.

But Bowie started to withdraw, shortly after 'Young Americans'. He was leaving them to it but to what, exactly? The Glen Miller revival, as practised by a group of retrophiliac kids on Canvey Island, all sporting wartime perms and close-tailored jackets? The Steve Harley/Cockney Rebel chainstore look? Or *Punk*?

Steve Strange
and Rusty Egan
with Visage.

Punk broke in 1976, with the Pistols scandalizing Bill Grundy and the nation, which was all very well as a diversion, but... what if you were David Bowie's spiritual child? What if Bryan was your lodestar? How did you really feel about mass punk, low punk grotesquerie – spitting and snotting and falling over and beating your brains out in an anti-style, anti-aspirational, angry, depressive, *ugly* mass movement? How was *that* going to make you reach for the stars?

Alternatives

So everything was poised, in waiting at the end of 1978. Then a club called *Billy's* opened up in Meard Street, in the thick of Soho, with all its desperate sex'n'novelty shops and its haggard doorways. In the middle of this, in a usually for-gays-only little *boîte*, a couple of boys took over on Tuesday nights and played some records for their friends and called it Bowie Night… and everyone with the Eye got to hear of it and something was in the air.

Not punk, for sure. Punk was the *problem*. Not that it wasn't, well, *refreshing* to hear those sounds crashing through at the end of 1976 and all through the following,

Jubilee, year. And it took the focus of attention firmly away from stadium antediluvians like Queen and the Eagles, and moved it back into the art schools and little colleges and onto the streets and estates. But it came with huge drawbacks.

For a start, the music was the wrong kind of music: *deliberately* awful, irritating music a lot of it (which, after all, made only a negligable commercial impact on the product being shifted by Boney M and Hot Chocolate) swiftly imploding into several little sub-orders, ranging from the 'poppest' Blondie to the indescribable Sham 69 and their BM skinhead followers. Not only couldn't you dance to most of it, you couldn't do much *else* to it, either, except perhaps mutilate yourself. It was ugly, and it attracted ugly people using madhouse imagery. Punk needed saying and it looked like the End of the World. But if you were in the gutter, did you really want to be reminded of it every waking hour? Ordinary poor kids didn't like it and style freaks soon became bored.

And there was another thing about Punk; there was something politico about it, something skirting the boundaries of social theory about it. It took on the initial symptoms of a serious movement, with all the dour, middle-class sensibility and dreary prescriptiveness that that entailed. Culture commentators and sociology professors were keen on Punk, even to the extent of… apeing some of the styles… these terrible, middle-class people, going out and copping a short haircut, a Help-the-Aged second-hand jacket, a skinny tie… even worse, far worse, there were some *American* groups trying to get in there.

You wanted to be *beautiful,* what on earth could you *do*? It was no use looking to David and Bryan, now. Yes, David had made his 'Low' album, which was wonderful in its way, and Bryan was well, Bryan was working. But really, David had scaled things down and was slightly off our planet anyway, while Bryan, clearly knocked back a bit by Punk, was working out how to get round his shocking Pop Dinosaur label.

A Small Seismic Shift

And then Billy's came along and kick-started the next wave. Two singular boys Steve Strange and Rusty Egan, who'd been hanging around for a couple of years, as part of the, London, fashion edge of punk, took over Gossips, a little Soho gay club, on Tuesday nights. Being London, and more relaxed than New York, the gay club scene generally was more open, more accessible to what you might call 'alternative' people; boys, girls, anyone who wanted to do things a little differently. So the style children always went down to the popular gay clubs and that was fine. And then Steve and Rusty put on a little party every Tuesday night for their friends – basically, St Martin's

Art School types, some University of London/London School of Economics people, kids from the suburbs and the estates – and they played the kind of music that no one had ever played before at a club.

They played German and Japanese techno-music, stuff with a disco beat but with a curiously inhuman, *shiny* finish to it. Kraftwerk were like the House Band – they never actually *went* there, of course – making strange, hissing, self-consciously robotic records and going along with the whole art school, self-absorbed, distanced deal by putting on pancake make-up and Weimar Republic hats for their publicity shots. So self-consciously cool and distanced were Kraftwerk from their own music, they sometimes put dummies in the musicians' places and let the sequencers and synths do the rest.

Which Is Where The Posers Come In

It was just perfect for the boys and girls: music that fitted in, rather than music which insisted on itself; music that was detached, self-aware, a little ironical. No anger, here, no *message*: just a soundtrack for style.

Perfect, too, was the little gay *boîte*. These kids weren't interested in *clubland* – some kind of hideous, lardy confection of chrome and spotlights and nook-and-cranny tables and all the Croydon-comes-to-the-West-End tat of your standard nightclub ambience. The more basic and improvized the setting (and your little gay *boîte* was necessarily a trifle underfunded in these departments), the less there was to distract from the performers, namely the members – style-fixated kids from the estates and the professional visualists and commentators from colleges in town, who turned up and lived the life… Wearing Weimar Republic black-tie outfits, pill-box hats, boas, Cossack vestments and pantomine Turkish trousers (like Bowie before them), Ruritanian Toy Soldier outfits, yards of satin, and *make-up* (both sexes) applied with 100 per cent freedom and relish.

There was no money in it, of course. You had to scrape all this stuff together with a dole cheque or a college grant or some kind of nothing work in a shop or for the council or whatever. If you were poor, you wore your wealth on your back. You turned yourself into an art object. And while Rusty worked the turntables, Steve worked the door, making sure that standards were maintained. The combination of the London Irish chancer with the young Winston style and the funny looking

The Blitz club – Tuesday night is dress-up night.

Back in 1980, two obscurely beautiful boys stand in the doorway of a squat in Carburton Street: George and Marilyn explore dress options shortly before assaulting the world with their own certainties.

Welsh, butcher's boy with the panto outfits worked; whatever anyone thought of them they offered a rallying point and they were energetic. They *wanted* a lot.

What would get you in that door? Being a member of the party, of course. Being a member of the inside group, opposed to the obvious youth movements that claimed you, conventional approaches, mainstream trendiness, but instead, individualistic, self-supporting, convinced of your instincts, dogmatically certain that We are It.

And if this sounds vaguely familiar, then yes: these cold little fishes, these *fabulous nobodies*, were behaving with the same absolutism, the same chilly élitism as the middle-aged suits struggling for the soul of the next government. Like them, the boys and girls saw themselves not as part of a social mass, community, but as brightly individual egos, using a collective setting to get the point across that they were all as *different* and *self-determining* as a turn-of-the-century congress of anarchists.

Except that anarchism wouldn't have done, not in a million years: too idealistic, too punky, too abstract. These people were *completely on the make*; materialists, apolitical, keen to turn events into opportunities… little guided missiles, seeking targets… like Sherman and Hoskyns and Joseph… *two clubs with a door policy*.

Coming Into Focus

There was something in the air. By this time, Rusty and Steve, having fallen out with the owner of Billy's, had talked their way into another Tuesday nighter, this time in a fading wine bar close to the Central Masonic Hall, off Covent Garden. They called it the Blitz Club and it opened its doors at the end of 1979. The turn of the decade.

Bigger and better, Steve Strange (his invented name from 1977, a provincial idea of the exotic) was on the door, Rusty played Kraftwerk and 'Low', Boy George was the cloakroom attendant, Marilyn, a fashionable teenage transvestite from the suburbs admired by louche artists, was a mascot, Spandau Ballet's manager saw the potential and made them the house band, Stephen Linard made the clothes, Robert Elms, still a student, wrote it up and Janet Street-Porter, always on the stroke, made a film about it. This was the first great fancy-dress party of the eighties. There would be thousands more, but this was the *first*. It had the whiff of legend about it the moment it started. Like seeing the Pistols in 1976, or being on the Boat in 1977, being a Blitzkid in 1980 was one of those terribly defining things.

Money & Fame

And it was all driven along by a strange new mix of fantasy, style yearning, preciousness and entrepreneurial zeal. Now *that* was something else: the way these boys and girls simply couldn't be bothered with the conventional approaches into Musicland – find some backers, see if you can get the A & R men to turn up, do it the normal way – instead they worked out a completely different strategy, involving contacts, networking, an awful lot of self-reliance, and an instinct for DIY publicity. They had no ideological baggage whatsoever.

Entrepreneurial zeal. As John Ranelagh notes in *Thatcher's People*, 'Entrepreneurs, notably in the fashion and pop culture worlds, only began multiplying in the 1970s. The pop and fashion worlds provided nearly all of Britain's success stories in that decade.' However grim things were got between 1979 and 1981 (and those were the years when the number of people out of work doubled to well over 2 million), it was clear that this group was going to do what it wanted anyway. Partly, it was because this was the last time anyone could surf into any kind of college on a straight student grant – so make the most of it – and conversely because they were realistic enough to understand that soon they were going to have to do some fairly serious hustling, not least because they were a load of obsessives, fanatics, dream believers.

But quick to spot an opportunity. When Charles Fox, the Covent Garden theatrical costumier, held its closing-down sale, the Blitz crowd descended in one fluid movement and bought up everything glamorous, old filmie, that it could find. Steve Strange and Stephen Linard bought a pair of matching ankle-length wolf-fur coats for five pounds each. When the Big world started to take them up and invite the Blitz kids to flavour up their own parties, the Blitz kids said thank you very much, did their stuff – i.e. acted up for the host – then disappeared into the night. At Paul Raymond's party, they stayed about half an hour, before returning with carrier bags full of chicken and salmon. *They worked at it.*

And the more they worked at it, the higher the stakes got. It went full circle when David Bowie, their inventor, asked Strange to supply people with the Look for his

Immaculate in tartan, Spandau Ballet made a design statement.

Pantomime dandy highwayman, Adam offered yet another retrospective take on the world. Old was new, borrowing was a sweet psychosis, the dressing-up cupboard had been broken open and its doors had been ripped off. This was British post-Modernism *for real.*

'Ashes To Ashes' video. Clearly and awesomely, the Mountain coming to Mohammed. Mick Jagger appeared and was famously refused admission by Steve Strange, the doorman of the New age: the man for whom nothing Old was admissable, for whom only the New would do. This was a major New Order declaration (in fact, rather prosaically, it was fire regulations). *Two clubs with a door policy....*

Here Comes The Past...

And if the New meant raiding the dressing-up box of English heritage and the Saturday afternoon, old TV movie heritage and making a whole different take on the Old, then that was the way now. With mordant symbolism, the Old Covent Garden re-opened as the New Old Covent Garden: the flower girls long gone, the lamp-brackets and ironwork lovingly coated in metal preservative and fresh paint, the stones and bricks brought back to life by a thousand hands in June 1980. It said to the world: this is where

we are now; theme park meets late night shopping mall meets true heritage. A Designer World, where the real looks fraudulent and the fake – the gift shops and the olde-worlde scent bowers – look authentically cynical.

Welcome to the New World, where even the original Covent Garden was re-invented as a holiday pastiche of itself.

It worked for Covent Garden, and it worked down at Blitz, where Stephen Linard was giving Spandau Ballet a re-think for their first video. Out went the patent dancing pumps and the white socks and in went *tartan*: kilts, sashes, billowing white Highlandy shirts, cross-gartering. So much for post-war England! Where we come from, the eighteenth century look works fine. And two weeks later, they were selling replica tartan sashes in Top Shop in Oxford Street.

... And Here Comes A Merchandising Opportunity

But then, weren't the Spandaus supposed to be a pop group? Leading edges. All that? Well, only in a sense. The Spandau rhetoric was that they were the same as the people they played for, sharing the same sensibilities, the absolutism of it all, the cliqueish-

ROBERT ELMS

Writer

Q What did you want in the late Seventies?

A I think I wanted to not live in a place that looked like Bulgaria. I think, most of it was negative; we lived in this nation which was grey beyond endurance, was corporate… and really did feel like Eastern Europe.

Q So who else was doing the wanting?

A I think we occurred in all sorts of places. We… were essentially working class, I'll say boys, because it was predominantly, homosexual and heterosexual male. I think we saw ourselves in that mod sense as the working class aristocrat, the Face, if you like.

Q So how did you and that band of brothers get together?

A I think that band of brothers occurred in all sorts of places. It occurred in Essex and they all wanted to go and get jobs in the City and wear red braces.

Q So they did.

A And so they did, and God bless them for it. And in some ways we had similar aspirations, but instead of the City we were aiming at Soho… Also our level of sophistication altered. I think there was a period in Britain when we'd become so divorced from everything. In Europe they had cappuccino and nice clothes, and all of those kinds of things. We didn't have any of that… and yet suddenly when we had

things like the Blitz we were ten years ahead, because we had this thing that everybody else wanted.

Q You, you and yours, I'm thinking of the collective you here, thinking of all those things that you ushered in, how did you do it?

A Well we did it by not knowing. Because England never knew anything, didn't know you couldn't make magazines, it didn't know you couldn't start nightclubs. It didn't know you couldn't do any of these things. So people did do stuff, people went out and started nightclubs. People went out and started magazines. People did clothes collections… No one believed you could do that in England in the late seventies. That was done by corporate bodies. We lived in a corporate nation, and for these kind of cheeky nineteen-year-olds with too much energy and too much to say and silly clothes on, to start things was preposterous. But we didn't know it was preposterous. If we had done, the weight of it might have stopped us doing anything, but we didn't. And so people formed bands that suddenly were on Top of the Pops. And there was one day when Steve Dagger said to me, 'I'm managing a band.' I said, 'what?' He said, 'oh yeah, you know, I've got a band. You come up with a name. You write the first review, we'll be a famous pop group, you'll be a writer.' They were Spandau Ballet, I was me, it worked. And there was extraordinary cheek about it. And providing you had that level of cheek, you could pull it off.

ness, the tasteful working-class exclusivity. They were as fastidious about clothes as they were about interesting venues, as about their first Germanic sets and stylizations. Their manager, Steve Dagger, didn't want them in the Marquee Club or the pages of the NME (the grey world of the musos). Instead, he advertised the gigs in Smile, the Chelsea hairdressers, in the shops that sold the St Martin's people's designs. Spandau played warehouses, the old Scala Cinema, HMS *Belfast*... HMS *Belfast*: this vast World War Two battlecruiser moored on the Thames up by Tower Bridge, was one of *the* gigs, where people suddenly turned up from all over the country, acting in their own private movie, dressed like stars on poverty rations, *hundreds* of them, so many that hundreds more were turned away.

Somewhere along the line, magazines started calling it the New Romantic look. And that was it: the first fashion cult since punk (and with full commercial crossover potential) was born. A powerful mixture of magpie retro, fastidious taste (it was hard to wear the look if you were a true-born slob) and market exploitation, tailor-made for what they were calling the art form of the eighties. The Blitz crowd was starting to go national. The closed circle was turning into a network of *operators*.

Start the club; *become* the group; *control* the presentation: all through *design, design, design* – you can do *all that*. The Blitz showed you how and the copyists moved right in. At the end of 1980, Cabaret Futura started up, more pretentious, if it were possible, featuring a mess of talents, egomaniacs and no-hopers, with the nascent Soft Cell and Depeche Mode somewhere on stage. Early in 1981, the Birmingham rum Runners Club boys, Duran Duran, sporting the full New Romantic kit (sunset hair colours, frilled blouses, leather britches, headbands) – Birmingham High Street version – appeared with 'Planet Earth'. The Blitz people said privately that they were hopelessly naff and provincial.

At the same time, Steve Strange invented his own, wholly absurd, group, Visage (names after Steve's heavy make-up habit) and made 'Fade To Grey', before moving out of the Blitz at the peak, starting new clubs: Hell (also in Covent Garden), Club For Heroes (Baker Street) and finally attracting big backers and giving the world the Camden Palace, a disused Camden Town theatre made into a colossal club of clubs, bigger, louder, more complicated than anything before. Adam Ant, another punk veteran of 21, had a major makeover in the new mode (from Malcolm McLaren, who knew a development opportunity when he saw it) and came back wearing dandy eighteenth-century highwayman's kit and a Sony Walkman on *Top Of The Pops*. The country was starting to go up in riots – St Paul's, Toxteth, Brixton – having convulsions as it left the past behind under the Iron Will of Mrs Thatcher, but Lady Diana Spencer looked right in a gold label, semi-Romantic get-up and she liked Duran Duran. At least the *haberdashery* of the early eighties was in place.

And all from a little gay *boîte* hosting a Bowie night for misfits on those cold, empty Tuesdays....

We Could Be Heroes

There was even a house magazine: *The Face*. In fact, *The Face* was how the rest of the world got to know that the Blitz generation had arrived and the party had started. Robert Elms, a LSE student, with his friend, Spandau Ballet's manager, Steve Dagger, saw the potential as Blitz insider columnist. Luckily for him, Nick Logan, the former editor of *New Musical Express*, was starting up *The Face* and wanted somethign to attach it to – a momentum; a movement.

Elms supplied that in spades: insider knowledge, total user-friendliness. One of his first pieces was 'The cult with no name', a movement focussed on his friends the Spandaus, lavishly photographed in various states of absolute, unimpeachable, style self-awareness, with Elms' text taking a suitably arrogant line, explaining in unambiguous terms that the Spandaus and their people were something of a different order from your previous teen cults... From there on, *The Face* became a Publishing Event. Even though, as Logan recalls, the first year and a half were 'very, very hard', true faith and publicity won through. Which was all the more piquant when you consider how dreadful most style/fashion/scene magazines had been, up to that point. The late seventies had actually seen a sudden growth of little magazines a lot of them Sniffin' Glue-type punk fanzines, admittedly intended to capitalize on the fact that at last something seemed to be happening. At the swank end of the trade, however, Andy Warhol's *Interview* provided the template, but it didn't seem to travel properly.

The result was a raft of aspirational 'style' magazines like *Deluxe, Boulevard, Frizz,* Bailey & Litchfield's *Ritz* and *Mode Avantgarde*, all amazingly lumpen lash-ups, full of hairdressers and tacky, drooling, sub-personality profiles which used the word 'Malibu' apparently without irony. They desperately wanted *glamour – Alternative Vogue* for swingers – but they looked crass. They were the journalistic equivalent of a

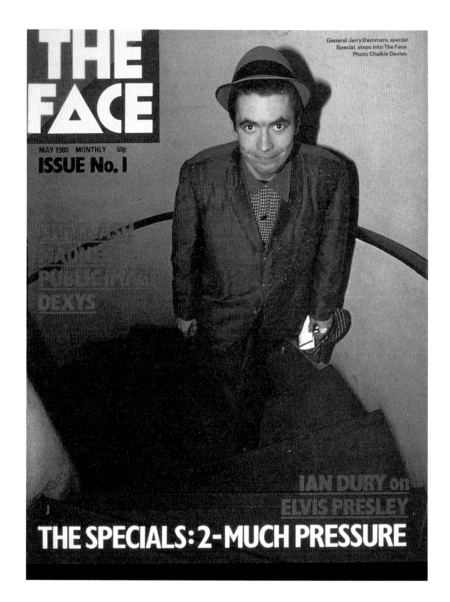

General Jerry Dammers, special
Special, steps into The Face.
Photo Chalkie Davies.

THE
FACE

MAY 1980 MONTHLY 60p
ISSUE No. 1

DEXYS

IAN DURY on
ELVIS PRESLEY

THE SPECIALS:2-MUCH PRESSURE

How it endures — while Adam and the Spandaus and George and Steve blossomed like desert flowers and then faded away, *The Face* said this is the way it will always be....

parked BMW with black windows. They were the sort of magazines that *liked* the idea of Mick Jagger.

The Face took nothing from any of that. Instead of starting in Kensington and working out, Logan an ex-Mod, still with a Mod's working-class style sensibilities and a feel for *writers,* gave it some edge. With art director Neville Brody, Logan defined the look of magazines for the eighties: spare, clean, retro-Modern, clever, knowing, catching the reader off the beat. The first cover portrait was Jerry Dammers, of the austere Specials (still a bit seventies, still finding a style). A few issues later, they did the New Romantics. *The turning point...* 'I wanted,' says Logan, 'to make a *Tatler* for a mass audience...'.

After that issue, the nationals took it up as a key 'feed' and we had the first *style* diary of the New Age, followed in 1980 by *i-D*, a rather more neo-Hippy middle-class strand of *style* and *individualism,* but all of it making it absolutely clear that *design* was the issue.

Plotters & Posers

These were the defining moments: when the outsiders got together and, with all that desperate arrogance and exclusivity of the shunned, decided to plot their own Brave New World. Let's not get too rapturous about it mind you. It wasn't as if John Hoskyns ever breezed down to Billy's or Blitz (although his boy, Barney, worked on the NME and rejected his dad's world then) just to see whether the new generation was likely to be receptive to his ideas. But both groups, the Plotters gathered around Thatcher and the Posers congregated around Steve Strange's clubs, had – instinctively or rigorously – arrived at the same conclusion: *there was nothing to lose.* The Right-wing theorists who'd made New Think workable, electable, were laying the political and economic foundations for the new decade. While a bunch of dandified metro-politan misfits were setting an egotistical style-*consciousness* which was to last well after the first phase of New Romantic had faded through Miss Selfridge.

When it came for Steve and the Blitz boys and girls, it was their right. For Alfred Sherman and the CPS, it was their struggle rewarded. Oddly enough, the two together turned into the 1980s.

P A R A D I S E

It all comes down to money. In the beginning and at the end, cash is what it's all about. We were just a bunch of Viv Nicholsons between 1982 and 1990: spend, spend, spend. *Of course we were: we'd never had that kind of money before.* Nor, come to think of it, had we had the right kind of taste guidance, or big enough windows on the world of good things, showing us the way to spend it, even if we'd had the cash in the first place. Nor did we have the right mood, the right sense of can and can't. No, to get the eighties effect took quite a lot of things coming together; the right time, right place, right people, right feelings, right fistfuls of cash. This wasn't *just* a consumer boom. Yes, we did go out and buy more – more TVs, more VCRs, state-of-the-art hi-fis, etc. – but it was really a new generation of consumerism with changes in advertising, retailing, financing, attitudes and expectations. And it's *still with us*: it set the pattern for the next ten or fifteen years. It was a complicated business.

Let's deal with the staff of life, first. Let's sort out the cash. Now, there are two things you have to remember about ready money: how much have you actually got and, just as important, *how do you feel about it*?

Go On, Help Yourself

Taking the readies first: the main things about the eighties were that we borrowed like maniacs and we took home more money, too, in a wages boom that really got going from 1982 onwards.

The borrowing side was taken care of in all sorts of ways: financial deregulation meant the banks were allowed to lend money on properties; and the building societies were allowed to lend *more* money, and on things that *weren't* properties. From 1986, the building societies could also offer you a cheque account and masses of other banking services, which meant that the banks and building societies (who had barely acknowledged each other's existence up to 1979) found themselves competing more and more frantically for the same customers. All that Listening Bank, Bank That Likes To Say Yes carry-on really dated from that time. On top of that, hire purchase restrictions had been abolished in 1982, and by the mid-eighties, the credit card boom (remember the days when a credit card account was free? Those were the days.) was well under way. The net indebtedness of householders by 1989 was two and a half times higher than it had been in 1982. Stir into this mix the fact that average real wages increased by 20 per cent between 1983 and 1987 and you can see that the money was, well, just about free.

What made it still sweeter, was the way we felt about it. The way you feel is the way you spend. And one of the great mood-enhancers of the period, was the tax cut. Everyone knows that basic rate income tax went down between 1979 and 1989 – from 33 per cent to 25 per cent. And we know that personal allowances went up (by 25 per cent) and, above all, that top rate tax (you lucky people) went down from 83 per cent to 40 per cent. At the same time, of course, irksome little things like national insurance contributions and VAT tended to take more of the tax slice in ways which weren't quite so visibly advertised, so that overall, the amount of tax most people paid didn't shrink as fast as the reduction of income tax suggested it would. But that didn't matter: the genius of the tax cut philosophy was that it got the party mood going, it got us all *glowing*. When Lawson did that little trick in his Budget speech in 1986, it was a *hoot*: 'I do not have the scope this year for a reduction in the basic rate of income tax' – takes sip from glass beside him, waits for Opposition catcalls, *told you so*, to die down – 'beyond one penny in the pound'. *Oh, neat*!

You've Worked For It...

And that's where the top rate tax reduction comes in. Given that most people were never going to find themselves paying the top rate, what did they care if the rate was halved? But we all have these ludicrous, overheated fantasies; these visions of ourselves in some scented future where we *will* have hit paydirt and we *will* be smothered with wealth in the back of some presidential Merc, somewhere. And if that were to happen, then it was just as well we wouldn't have to pay more than 40 per cent income tax on the wedge. It was going to encourage Enterprise. The tax man shared our dreams – he really did. It made us all feel *good* about getting and spending and not being ashamed any more.

In some cases personal wealth rose by 80 per cent in real terms in the 1980s. *Eighty per cent*. Between 1982 and 1989, the average growth of personal consumption was 4.6 per cent a year, almost double what it had been in the twenty years leading up to Thatcher. As Peregrine Worsthorne so movingly wrote in a *Sunday Telegraph* editorial, 'Lots of people today, particularly young people, are bent on making money. But making money is not evil or sinful or doing the devil's work.' *Hallelujah!*

Consumption: now that's another order of experience, another matter altogether. Naturally enough, getting will tend to go hand-in-glove with spending; but spending is a cultural activity as well as an economic one. The way you spend is as important as how much you spend. So where do we get our ideas of the way to spend?

To begin with, it's in the air, it's all around us, we see what everyone else is doing and we recall what they did in the past, and that gives us something to go on. Not an eighties phenomenon, of course: the rise and rise of the consumer had actually been going since the mid-fifties; and by the early seventies was both full of potential, and nicely matured at the same time. Way back in, say, 1972, you could find all the totems of an advanced consumerist society – foreign holidays, small luxury items (whiskies, scent, fancily packed cigs), colour TVs, credit cards, hi-fi innnovations (the heady days of quad sound), fancy clothes for men and women – all the good things of life. The You've-Earned-It belief and all that I-Want-More aspiration weren't simply inventions of the eighties, no matter how much it seems that way.

The Dismal Decade

And yet, by the end of the seventies, the consumerism train had been derailed. The individual spender had lost out, somewhere. He didn't seem to count for much as he used to. A lot of the late seventies spending seemed to be corporatist spending, the invisible kind which either happens so slowly it becomes part of the landscape, or happens behind closed doors and usually to someone else. It was the opposite of consumerism, because no consumers seemed to be involved. Government, industry, the unions: they certainly had the funds, and they were certainly spending them. But the immediate, tangible benefits were hard to come by. Individuals, on the other hand, either didn't have the cash, or if they did, they didn't want to make a big deal about their spending it. Ostentation wasn't an option. If you had money, you kept quiet about it.

Nor were there any great consumer role models in the seventies – instead of getters and spenders, we had a raft of ageing corporatist figures (Lord Stokes, James Callaghan, Len Murray, Lord Thomson of Fleet); some half-baked media favourites (Terry and June, Michael Parkinson, Jason King, Tony Blackburn), some classic losers (Citizen Smith, Frank Spencer and Basil Fawlty) and, as time went by, one or two very *angry* fellows (Trevor Griffiths, John Lydon, Tony Parsons), to set a countervailing tone of disgust.

It was scarlet and it was gold – the colour of money – and it was Chanel and it was 1988. Who could want for anything more?

If you couldn't afford the suit, you could still have the accessories.

The aristocracy (such as it was) was still well entrenched after a decade of socialism (remember Jubilee Year, 1977? The nation fell in with that glorious flim-flam without a qualm, just as if it were the Coronation and we were hurrahing Edmund Hilary and the Canberra bomber and free teeth and spectacles). But like most British institutions, the upper classes were just that bit shabbier, just that bit less inspiring than they had been a generation before. The idea of toffs setting any consumer trends in 1975 would have been risible to a degree. Equally, the chattering classes – the kinds of people who manned the broadsheets and public service television – whatever it was they stood for then, *it wasn't the sharp looks or getting and spending*. Politically, we were heading for a showdown; materially, we were living compromised lives. The poverty of our desires, you might say.

The other problem was that so much of what we could buy, was dismal. We lived in a world of brown, chalkstripe, Take 6 suits; dumb TVs in big, teak-effect boxes; popular cars which – despite the consumerist additions of goodies, extras and bits of flash over the years – were flimsy and rotten to drive; food which was utilitarian and unexciting, no matter how hard the PR people tried to persuade you it was a gastro-nomic experience. So much of the consumer experience (which should have been so *rich*, so *pleasurable*) was stuck in a brownish-greyish morass of inadequacy. It was all through the seventies that we began to realize how badly designed and manufactured British goods were, while at the same time, not having absolute access to all those German and Japanese goodies that were waiting just across the waters. A BMW was *rare* in 1975.

And underneath all this was yet another kind of discontent: even though things did change a bit and were updated from time to time in a typically British, under-fund-ed, ill-thought-through fashion, there was this sense that nothing much had moved on from the decades before. We'd got used to these things, these cars, TVs, washing machines, hi-fis, casual slacks, holidays in Malta, cream sherries, Italian-style light fittings: they were being touted as luxury goods, but in fact they'd become *basics*, stuff you took for granted, the wallpaper of existence. When your folks bought a TV in the fifties, the whole street knew about it. By 1975, the only remarkable state of affairs was *not* having a TV.

So what happened to change this melancholy state of affairs? Who taught us how to *desire*?

Enter A Different World

The print media were in on it from the start. Leaving aside for the time being your existing minority islands of imported luxury – *Harpers & Queen, Vogue* and *Tatler* – what the eighties did see was the rise and rise of soft journalism, journalism which took the national papers away from hard news and current affairs, and more into features, profiles, lifestyle matters, and especially, 'service features' – information about what to do and buy. Over the decade, the line between editorial and advertising became increasingly fuzzy. There evolved a pretty seamless relationship between the world of features and the world of desirable commodities. It didn't matter if the tone of the editorial was critical, approving, blandly informative or making use of lovely and desirable artifacts as part of a larger argument: the fact of the matter was that for a lot of the time, editorial and advertising were talking about the same things. The word 'advertorial', a pormanteau of two once mutually exclusive activities, become a commonplace. Not only that, but the papers were relatively less inclined to compromise the advertising which filled their pages by getting into hard-hitting stuff about disease, poverty, the environment and what have you; and were more inclined to run interviews with and profiles of, the stars (or failing that, the personalities) emerging into the daylight of the decade.

Consider what you were likely to get in a newspaper colour magazine in the early mid-sixties and compare it with what you got, twenty years later. In a *Sunday Times Colour Magazine* of 9 June 1963, you got (a) an enormously long and *solid* piece about NATO and Polaris, followed by (b) an enormously long and *solid* piece about the Cecil family. In the middle came (c) a double-page spread from Robert Carrier, telling us how to cook lentils. And that was it. But move up to 9 September 1984 and things have really changed: in the *Sunday Times Magazine* from that month, you found a long and *bitchy* article on the making of Francis Ford Coppola's *Cotton Club*, plus a long and *fawning* article about four well-connected women (including the Hon. Mrs Astor and the Duchess of Devonshire) and how they had interior-designed their altogether wonderful houses. Beat your way through a thicket of high-ticket ads – the magazine had more than doubled in size in the intervening years – and you came upon (for the heavyweight readership) a profile of novelist Angela Carter. And bringing up the rear, you got a jolly little seal of approval for Safeway's Extra Virgin Olive Oil (because Extra Virgin Olive Oil was *news* in 1984).

Not convinced, yet? Try it again: on 16 February 1964, you could read about the Boy Scout movement, General de Gaulle's wife and Michelangelo, as seen by Henry Moore. Good but… *sensible.* Cut to 7 December 1986, and we have a big spread on fur coats (still – just – fashion items, rather than hate objects), a piece on the fall and rise of the British finishing school (seriously), big pix on Bertolucci's *Last Emperor,* plus something on a charm school for bouncers, closed off by a very user-friendly survey of automatic cameras. Oh, and three times as many pages. This is the *Sunday Times*: the crusading, heavyweight *Sunday Times.* Anyone remember the crusading, heavyweight *Sunday Times*? It doesn't matter.

We are talking about a whole change of mood, of tone. Make it big on colour, make it big on fun, make the newspaper of the eighties read like an upmarket magazine had ten years earlier. And in doing it, make everyone feel, *I want a piece of that.* Obviously, it kept the advertisers happy; but it also connected with those pent-up yearnings for Good Things, the real stuff (now affordable, of course) for *something better.* As Fleet Street decamped to Wapping and a new world of computerized typesetting, so it became cheaper to produce the papers and so the papers got bigger and bigger, splitting themselves up into more and more focused units – magazines and supplements – each a vehicle for highly targeted advertising, profiling, consumer surveys, lifestyle meditations – and very little in the way of hard news – which was, anyway, becoming more and more the province of the TV channels.

It took Eddy Shah to demonstrate that the papers could be colourful.

Remember when the *Sunday Times* – with Harry Evans and the crusading, heavyweight reputation long gone – screwed up over the Hitler Diaries? Did Rupert Murdoch care? As Evans observes in *Good Times, Bad Times,*

'When he was told that the diaries were fake, he reassured the worried editorial men at Times Newspapers who feared for their credibility: 'After all,' Murdoch said, 'we are in the entertainment business.' What was significant about the launch of *Today* newspaper in 1986? Not the fact that it was an entirely new title in a traditionally ossified market, nor the fact that it was a friendly, affordable, lower-middle tabloid for metropolitan commuters – it was the fact that it was *in colour* which made it worth noticing. When the *Independent* came out later in the same year one of its principal selling qualities – its high-class news gathering and informed, unbiased comment aside – was its *pictures*. People didn't just want a new, serious broadsheet – they wanted a good, serious broadsheet with entertaining, well-reproduced pictures. And the *Independent* swore to give them just that.

Let's Talk About Me

Perhaps the best example of the fourth estate's new passion for lifestyle and soft features was the *Mail On Sunday*'s *YOU* magazine, launched in 1982. The *Daily Mail*, under David English, was already setting the standards for pro-Tory, patriotic talk-it-up, middle-England tabloid journalism and had become an indispensible part of life for millions of lower and middle-middle-class new materialists who liked the idea of personal investment and a standard of living and had no liberal old shoe inhibitions about it. The Sunday *YOU* magazine – long on fashion, celebrity profiles, how-to hedonism and eighties' cheek – built on that, dealing brilliantly with the entertainment business side of the national press, and setting the pace in *aspirant* (a key eighties marketing word) lifestyle voyeurism.

The first issue of *YOU*, the *Mail on Sunday*'s colour magazine, in October 1982. A new window on our lifestyle. 'Young middle-class aspires, go get'.

So successful was it that, in 1988, Associated Newspapers tried to do a *YOU* on the Saturday *Mail*, turning out another soft features/consumer interest/lifestyle colour supplement, called, unwinningly, *Male & Femail*. Well, It didn't work and was switched off after only a few months; while *YOU* goes on as ever. By 1988 there were so many titles fighting for the same advertisers that something had to give. And by the late eighties, we were all getting a little too sophisticated, a little spoilt for choice; we weren't going to be wowed by a supplement just because it was free, in colour and had Ivana Trump on the front cover. The magazines had educated their buyers, moved them light years in six.

Swanning around with
Elizabeth & Philip
Charles & Diana
Ronald & Nancy
Carolina & Reinaldo
Henry & Willie

Jumped-up June

Tina Brown's first *Tatler*: flash, snobbery, *fun* – all for just over a quid.

Only *Interiors*, launched in 1981, hit a hidden nerve more successfully. But while *YOU* was the full orchestra, big hits for the mass audience, *Interiors* was more like chamber music for materialists. 'Luxury is the footnote to his perfectionism,' is the sort of thing it said about its featured aesthetes. Edited by Min Hogg, orchestrated by Kevin Kelly, *Interiors* was a journey to the new frontier of consumption – the fabulously atmospheric interior in tune with the obsession, the economic engine of the decade, *domestic property*. it managed to make rich people's interior decoration sound something like an artistic quest. These were the secret houses of the seriously rich and the durably famous. It was brilliantly done, the more so in never looking like advertorial in those first years. Although the editorial told you in no uncertain terms what to want, it hardly ever told you where to get it, or, assuming you could get hold of the pictures and furniture like that, how to get it looking just so.

The more mature glossies – *Vogue, Tatler* and *Harpers & Queen* – continued to provide the same reassurances, the same guidance. They just put on readers at a lick. Lovely new money meant hundreds more spenders needing help on the nursery slopes of serious spending. *Tatler* in particular, went from being an embarrassment – an old title bought and sold and constantly, badly revived – to being a definitive guide to the decade. Tina Brown moved Tatler clearly into the global celebrity culture, where the equivalence and the conjunction of a duke and a movie star were self-evident. Life as a party, life as a film set. The new society she described was straightforwardly ambitious, not deferential. It was the Next Step. And as a result, the most unlikely people started clutching *Tatlers* in public and checking out Bubbles Rothermere's private life and Alastair Little's restaurants and yellow cords from Hackett. *Tatler* became a source-book, a repository of consumer ideas and styles in a way which would have been inconceivable ten years earlier.

The Pick And Mix Life

Just like *The Official Sloane Ranger Handbook* (to give it its proper title). A *strange business*, the *Sloane Ranger Handbook*. Published in 1982, it looked at first sight like a Christmas spoof, a funny book. But it was really two books: the really funny bits were the pictures, which said it all by catching the style exactly, and could be seen, by those who cared to, as in some way 'revealing' or 'satirical'. And then there was *the text*. It was incredibly informative. It was an anthropologist's textbook (the hidden tribe; the society within a society) and, even more tellingly, it turned out to be an aspirant's guidebook.

Seriously: things were just on the move in 1982, that let's-buy-ourselves-a-lifestyle feeling was just starting to infect the nation's consciousness and turn into a fever… and Sloanes were the perfect models, upper middle-classy (Sloanes enjoyed nice new consumables like BMWs and expensive holidays as well as old houses in the country), not wholly unrecognisable (amazing how many of us turned out to know the odd Sloane or near as dammit) yet wonderfully, Englishly old-fashioned. Buy that 1860s house, do it up in your own retro mish-mash (courtesy of *Interiors* magazine and B & Q) and stand in front of your repro/salvaged/nicked Neo fireplace, wearing a tweed jacket. With a how-to book and a little cash, aspirants could escape the Human Condition, could play-act, be someone entirely new. Had Ann Barr and I thought all this through

when we proposed the book in 1981? I'd love to say we had, but it was all more inno-
cent than that, a lot provoked by the way the Princess of Wales had seized the national
imagination.

This was something which the subsequent rash of me-too handbooks (for New
Georgians, foodies, whatever) never quite caught onto – the handbook as lifestyle
primer and shopping list. While there was real desperation to spend money, eighties
aspirants needed to feel that what they were buying was going to be *the real thing*, an
investment. Foodies and Georgians were all very well, but for one reason or another, most
people didn't want to *be* them. They didn't want quite that level of detail, of commitment. They'd had too many years of thwarted consumerism and shoddy goods behind
them, to wait any longer. They wanted to spend real money immediately on something
which was quality, but which also fitted deeply into the cluttered English psyche: once
they'd got that equation sorted, it was out with the Amex card and on with the gear.

To take another example, in another medium: *Brideshead Revisited* versus *Capital
City*. *Brideshead* came out in 1981 and for all its faults holds a place in the romantic
middle-class heart because, let's be honest, we could all do with a bit of that ourselves.
Oxford, having some of *the set* ready to hand as it were, makes a habit of rediscover-
ing *Brideshead* every ten years or so; on this occasion, everyone else got a look in at
the same time – and didn't we like what we saw? Pure end-of-an-era style; great set-
tings, great clothes, great snobberies. Granada TV may have intended it as a faithful
adaptation of Evelyn Waugh's best-selling novel, but it was *used* as a style catalogue,
just like the Sloane Ranger book. Why do you think Hackett took off the way it did?

Capital City, on the other hand, came out in 1989. It too, was drama with an
unmissable style catalogue subtext (City boys and girls, Armani clothing, BMWs,
mobiles and sub-Docklands apartments) but it didn't catch on. It was at the wrong
end of the decade for a start – out of date before it even got shown, with the crash of
1987 having put the City in question and out of fashion, and all that fixing and smart
restaurants and Young Guns and reach-me-down chic looking, well, a bit *silly*.
Especially since *Wall Street* had done it all better and earlier. On top of that, it was
peddling the wrong aspirations. The right aspirations were Sloane, the Royal
Wedding, our brave boys in the Falklands. There was nothing wrong with cordless
'phones and designer water, mind you, but they were too easy to come by. And if you
hadn't come by them by 1989, you weren't ever going to.

The Levis ad – Nick Kamen confirmed the body beautiful; and the essential rightness of boxer shorts.

Better Than The Programmes...

You didn't have to pick up your consumer cues from subtexts, handbooks or glossies, of course. You could get them straight. You could submerge yourself in that warm, nourishing bath which was advertising in the eighties. Ads have always been culturally important, of course – but in the spirit of the eighties, absolutely everyone acknowledged their importance. They were *crucial.* This was because there was so much more advertising. As well as a fresh swathe of colour publications to fill, there was Channel 4 (launched in 1982), longer and later programme schedules on ITV, morning TV, even Sky TV (launched in 1984, to a mass audience of 10 000 subscribers).

At the same time, the advertising agencies raised their game in every way, including producing some genuinely memorable campaigns, the kind which are contracted into catchphrases, which stand-up comics appropriate, and which other ads then rip off and use in a knowing, deconstructed fashion, the kind which people come to say are more entertaining than the programmes. The VW Golf that fell through the floor; the Levis ad with Nick Kamen taking off his jeans in the laundrette; the BT ads with Maureen Lipman; the other VW Golf retained by the cool, independent woman who gives back the fur coat and the jewellery; the massively memorable Milton Keynes campaign with children sending off red balloons (while the Broadwater Farm riots were played on the other channel); the Carling Black Label 'I bet he drinks…' campaign; a whole raft of Sainsbury's and Volvo ads from Abbot Mead Vickers, the quintessence of bourgeois aspiration; all those *Vorsprung durch Technik* commercials for Audi cars….

The Audi ads in particular, struck all sorts of chords with their audience. At the time (circa 1982), Audi cars had a fairly lamentable image amongst the British – not as *bad* cars, but because no one quite knew what they were or where they came from or what (if anything) was good about them. The very name, Audi, tended to mislead, sounding as it did, more Italian than German, more wimpish than power-dressed.

Then a new advertising agency, Bartle, Bogle, Hegarty (sic) won the account and started developing a positioning, a style for Audi, starting with the Audi 100. The first TV ad was bold, but problematic. It showed an aerodynamic Audi 100 whizzing through the desert, trailing parachutes behind it, to represent the order of wind resistance that a normal car would have experienced at the same speed. But the 'chutes fly off, the drag is overcome by the slippery 100 shape and the canny Audi driver zings off cleverly into the sunset. However, the Independent Television Contractors' Association decided that some parachutes ought to remain tied to the back of the car, since it was aerodynamic but not completely without some resistance to the air. So there you had it: a fairly aerodynamic car. So?

The next ad, however, was a complete cracker. This was the one where you barely saw the car – except at the end – and instead listened to Geoffrey Palmer at his most insinuating, going on about how the Schmidts, Mullers and Reinhardts all drive down to their summer villas, but only the Reinhardts are clever enough to do it economically and in style in their Audi and so on and so forth. A great ad, sales rose gratifyingly, everyone was happy. But it was more than that, more than the eighties' equivalent of Go To Work On An Egg.

First of all, it was extremely high-tone in concept and execution. It was superglossy to look at, a moving equivalent of two pages from *Harpers*. Without even showing the goods, its production values said that this was a quality enterprise, a serious, expensive, deluxe piece of business. Then, in its tantalizing use of close-ups and trick shots, and its concealment of the car till the end, it said to the viewers (rather, to the *partic-*

ular consumers it targetted), we know what you're like; you think you're pretty smart, don't you? Smart enough to get the joke and cinematic references, anyway. And last of all, with the pay-off of *Vorsprung durch Technik*, you got a brilliant encapsulation of the car's quality appeal – it's German, so it's going to be a good car. Why go out of your way to make a point which everyone knows already? Just say it's German: Teutonic branding will do the rest. It was a clever, austerely purposeful, well-thought-out ad which started the target buyer re-classifying Audi. The look, the execution, the irony – it was perfect.

And in that sense, it spoke for all the best advertising of the decade – advertising which implied wealth, sublime quality, consumer deliciousness, without having to load up the page or screen like the Christmas Grotto. It was also advertising which helped the viewer grow up pretty quickly – once you'd got the Volvo ads or the Sainsbury's ads or the Audi ads under your belt, you weren't going to look twice at the guff for those sixties-brand lighters or *rosé* wine, if it was just a page of slack feel-good copy with an obvious pack-shot.

It went without saying, that these ads, the best ads, were all predicated on the notion that what they were selling was actually a *quality* product. The real Stuff. Strange but true: we had become so used to the idea that advertisements were basically there to conceal the shortcomings of second-rate products, that it was a deeply refreshing reversal of principle to find that quite often – as the decade wore on – we were able to lay our hands on well-made things (German dishwashers; Japanese TVs) and little luxuries without too much stress. Advertising became less hard sell *and* less soft-sell and more subtly informative… with *attitude*. It was as if, instead of trying desperately to peddle you something you didn't really need, it was trying to inform you, trying to put new and valid options in front of you. It was trying to *educate* you.

The High Street University

And so, of course, were the shops. Good retailing has always been about adjusting expectations, creating what its ideological critics call the degraded theatre of goods. From the first days of Boots and Woolworths, to the early department stores – Bourne & Hollingsworth, Swan & Edgar and Debenham & Freebody – to Harrods and Harvey Nichols now, shops have educated and *added value*, either, like Boots and Woolworths, by proffering an Aladdin's cave of simple, affordable stuff under one, well-lit roof; or, like Harvey Nichols, by promising an experience, selling absolute confidence. Shops – the successful ones, at least – say to their customers, 'This is what it can be like.' And once you've had that experience, that perception of the way it can be, then you build on it and learn from it and expect something different from everyone else. Conran started as an educator with Habitat. But things took a jump up in the eighties. They moved on in a way which was qualitatively different, and which changed the way we bought.

Was it shopping malls? To some extent. Yes, in the obvious sense that they generated

These things *mattered*: The Design Museum proved it. You wanted it, you got it, and you took it home in something which was a statement on your whole lifestyle. The carrier bag as *desideratum*.

a whole new environment in which to shop, they dictated a new timetable to the act of shopping, they brought together as many different retailers as they could under one roof and created an atmosphere – an expectation – of superabundance, of critical mass. They did it on the grand scale, the Gateshead Metro Centre and Brent Cross, no less than their American progenitors. But did they actually change what we buy and the way we feel about buying it? Does the huge aggregation of retailers that is justification of any shopping mall actually change you? Or is it just another kin overweening consumer monotony, like cable TV or five different pizza parlours in the same high street?

No, you have to go down a level, before you find the real revolution. You have to get down to the retail unit. And frankly, you have to get down to Next.

This is how it went for George Davies and Next. George Davies, a former Ankle Sock Controller for Littlewoods, starts his own company, School Care, in 1971, selling 'total look' clothes for schoolchildren. School Care folds, Davies joins Pippa Dee ('clothing parties'), learns the virtues of co-ordinated clothing for women, gets fired from Pippa Dee in 1981 and gets taken on by Hepworths to re-work the Kendalls chain – which becomes Next in February 1982. *Big* hit. August 1984, launches Next for Men. October 1984 launches first mini-department stores, incorporating Next, Next for Men, a shoe department and a café. In 1985, Davies gets kiss of death: the *Guardian* Young Businessman Of The Year Award. From August 1985 to December 1988, launches Next Accessories, Next Interior, Next Cosmetics, Next Too, Next Collection, Next Boys & Girls, Next Directory, Next Originals, Next Jewellers, Department X, N24 Hours mail order and… is removed from the board of Next Plc, along with his wife Liz. Next then promptly cuts every cost in sight, closes thousands of square metres of loss-making space, ditches the Next Gardening Directory (how did that get in there?) and re-emerges, leaner, somewhat duller, but fitter. George Davies, meanwhile, writes his autobiography and looks for a suitable opening for his talents.

You have to try and remember what it was like before Next. It's almost impossible – now that half the High Street has gone for that all-worked-through, educational, co-ordinated style, everything set in warm, woody, quality environments (even M & S, God bless them) – but think back to 1979. In those days, clothes sat around on racks, in huge numbers, waiting passively for punters to come along and do the sums, try out the combinations. Dummies stood in the windows, looking like dummies. Shirts were with shirts, skirts with skirts, knitwear was off somewhere else altogether. Things were rigidly grouped by type, rather than by colour or co-ordinate potential. Shops obeyed a uniform age-and-class segmentation: a bit of tacky chrome and spot lighting for the young boutiques; a bit of furry wallpaper and some dubious emulsion for the middle-agers. Some shops sold some things you wanted, other shops sold other bits

INTERVIEW

GEORGE DAVIES

Creator of Next

Q What was the big idea back then at the beginning of 1982?

A A group called Hepworth bought sixty shops [and] in the year preceding 1982 myself and a team of people put a concept together and we thought that we could convert the sixties shops in about two months to make a very big impact on the high street and… give people what they believed they couldn't actually get… in very simple terms: affordable, stylish products at a value level that was somewhere pitched between M & S and Jaeger.

Q What kinds of aspirations do you think they had right then? What did you see them wanting?

A Well during, I think, the seventies early eighties there was a whole plethora of new magazines, ladies' fashion magazines particularly. So if people were buying magazines and in a sense educating themselves, not being a slave to a cat walk fashion… you knew that this consumer was becoming disconcerning…

Q Who were those people in your mind's eye, those aspirational people who wanted better?

A I certainly wasn't aiming at the fifteen/sixteen-year-old and, I suppose, in my mind I was among the early twenties, mainly because when we're over twenty our figure shapes change.

Q So that was what you wanted to do, how did you make sure it happened? What was really important about making Next real, making it work, keeping it different?

A Standards. I believe you've got to have standards and you've got to be unrelenting in your approach to standards and standards mean quality.

Q Tell me about the look of the shop, because Next had a very distinctive look. What was the point?

A Well, simplicity, the windows… did not have a model form in them, a bust, they were all flat dressing, but the flat dressing would have the belt, the skirt, the jumper, the shoes, not all in red, which might have been pretty simple, but offering a way of putting a collection it items together.

Q What was the image of Next and the image of its ideal customer?

A Well, I felt an image is about having a small piece of a person's mind, in other words, it's a recollection and the key thing was the consumer. Once they'd been into Next and saw how it… they left with a recollection, an image of a total retailing opportunity.

Q You've talked about your customers staying with you and buying new things. What do you think you did for those individual customers?

A You've tried to maintain the loyalty to your long term customers, and in a sense repay their loyalty [but] people get older… so, on one hand, you're trying to keep a statement to the person you had for many years, and yet the life blood of retailing is attracting new, younger people into your shop. So it's a very fine line.

and pieces; and if you were out of London (out of the centre of London, even), the real choice was pretty sad. High style was not High Street.

Terence Conran's Habitat – a sixties' invention – had the right idea – get it all under one roof, we'll show you how to put it together, let's make the shop look more like somewhere you'd want to live. But you couldn't get dressed at Habitat. And besides, Habitat wasn't everywhere – it served a very particular kind of educated new middle class and had never got much further north than Watford.

Looking The Part

No, the shock of entering your first Next, or your first Next for Men, was something altogether new. For the first time, quite possibly in your life, you had a retailer who could see inside your mind, who knew the look you wanted and the environment in which you wanted to stand while you shopped, who understood your dreams and brought them together in one place, at the right price, in your High Street. In 1982 we had the money and we wanted to dress up. We wanted that power outfit look, that killer bimbo look, that commercials-director-in-Covent-Garden look, that wide-shouldered, double-breasted, look-at-me-I'm-a-business-exec look. And while we might have glimpsed fragments of it here and there up to now, this was the first time we'd seen it done to the last detail, altogether, before our very eyes. We wanted to dress the part, and George Davies showed us how.

You could tell how acutely he'd read our dreams, by the fact that so many boys and girls flocked to the shops. Notionally aimed at twenty-five- to forty-year-olds (the people young enough to care but old enough to have the readies), Next sucked in teenagers and twenty-year-old babes, smart kids who wanted that look, that complete, worked-through, simple-but-sophisticated, grown-up, *non-tacky* look. And once Next for Men turned up in 1984, we could all feel that George had understood us – and that in itself was a liberation: the idea of the store being androgynous, purely a style source-book for Life. People even found themselves trying to get jobs at Next, just to be among the merchandise, to be *there*....

Davies made provincials with an eye feel that they'd come to the right place. He gave them aspirational clothes and he displayed them in a smooth, simple, coolly expensive setting – the equivalent of an Audi or a BMW: restrained, upmarket, *good taste*. No dummies in the windows for Next; things called waterfalls instead – plain,

D D A

Designed by
David Davies Associates
20 Bruton Street, London W1 01 631 5122

Store Design
Graphics
Packaging
Furniture

D D A

The shopping mall — a chance to explore out-of-town leisure/ retail options in comfort in the company of thousands like ourselves in a staged, hermetic *American* environment.

Consumerism meets evangelism meets aspiration. George Davies' gift to the world was quietly shocking... civilized, coherent. Next managed to dress almost everyone in Britain, while making us feel as if every buy was a matter of supremely individual choice, of design patronage.

INTERVIEW

RODNEY FITCH

Designer for retail outlets and commercial buildings

Q In the eighties, design was a rather popular word with clients and with customers. People all seemed to like the idea of things being designer something, but what were they actually getting out of it?

A I think they were getting reassurance Both clients, and through our clients' shops, the customers were getting reassurance. They were getting help, they were being nannied in a sense because they were being told what was progress. People were very insecure I think in stylistic terms in the eighties and through designers and designer brands I think they got a great deal of reassurance – in a sense what it was to be an eighties, stylish person.

Q So the designers' name became the sort of academy stamp: this is right, this is OK?

A Yeah, I think there's something in that and plainly the designer brand is one of the issues there. If you buy Next or Timberland, if you buy Reebok, what you are buying into are brand values, which have been established both stylistically and through the media and through communications, with which customers can identify and it's the retail designers' job to present those designer brands in an environment that is equally reassuring.

Q Now you looked very closely at Next, didn't you, because you were working for Next's competitors?

A Sure.

Q What was Next doing? What was the design role of Next?

A Next set themselves up as being the design style of the eighties and they carried that through outerwear, through to underwear, shoes, hats, everything and perhaps in so doing created a Next look which became rather dominant in the eighties.

Q So you could become a Nextie?

A Yeah, yes exactly, in the same way that remember in the sixties people became Habitatites – their homes were established and determined by the Habitat look.

Q Good taste on a plate.

A Yes, [you] don't have to think too hard about it, you don't have to put it together yourself.

Q What did retail design do for Next?

A Well I think it... helped set Next up as a kind of style-centre, it enabled Next, through the choice of materials, to create a kind of Next look which was reassuring, which was solid, which was understated middle-classness. It enabled Next to create a platform on which their principal idea of co-ordination could be traded.

Q When you say co-ordination, how did that work?

A Well, remember that Next sells a wide range of products. It sells all the things that you would need and the big, big issue I think in the eighties, for Next, was how to put these things together, how to have the right tie with the right shirt with the right waistcoat with the right jacket. In other words, how do you become an eighties person compliments of Next. And so the co-ordination became very very important, it also enabled Next to, what we call, cross-sell... I go in for a shirt, but because of the way the retail designer has presented the store I end up buying a shirt and tie, I go in to buy a jacket but because of the co-ordination in the presentation I end up buying the trousers that go with the jacket that I wanted. This sounds so simple now, but it was quite a revolution at the time because most stores at the beginning of the eighties actually sold their merchandise on the basis of category domination, i.e. I've got more trousers or I've got more jackets or, I've got more ties, than anybody else, but left you to make the decision – which tie, which jacket, which trousers? Next came along and said we don't pretend to have more trousers than anybody else but we have the right trousers that go with this jacket and look at this ensemble, and it worked.

Q Now you said Next created, or the designers created for Next, a feeling of reassurance and middle-classness. How did they do that in detail?

A Two factors I think, one was a sense of space. There was a sense of order, there was a sense almost of timelessness. Unlike most people's thinking, it wasn't a sort of hugely extravagant interior it wasn't crowded, it was calm and the second aspect of that, of course, is the materials; simple woods, nice pleasant metals, calm colours and, of course, the ubiquitous low-voltage lighting. No great fluorescent lights, no great flood-lights, just simple.

Q So did design raise peoples expectations more in the eighties than in the seventies, or the sixties? What did it set them up for, how did it all work?

A Well, a big question, but certainly eighties retail design did raise, and was intended to raise people's expectations, it was intended to add quality into their lives by making the shopping experience a pleasurable and interesting and vibrant one, rather than the dull experiences of the seventies.

Q So if you had a shop that looked quality, then you'd read quality into the product and in to the service.

A You'd read not only quality in to the product and the service, but I think you'd also read difference. If my client's store exuded a kind of quality and difference it set itself apart from the competition, and it attracted more customers than my competitor, and that is the object of the exercise.

Q What did those briefs from clients usually say? Number one, we want you to do this and this and this.

A Top of all of the briefs was: we must be different, this is a very competitive environment, and our look, our approach and our presentation must be different from the competition. Secondly, there was always a part of the brief which said the product itself is king, it is important, it is not just a question of shop fixtures and shop fittings, but how do those fixtures enhance the product, because at the end of the day, obviously it is the product that matters.

Forget architecture, forget graphics. 'Design' was the dynamic word for the decade and *Blueprint* had it all.

geometric cascades of wood, with the merchandise spread carefully across it like an invitation. All that light, warm wood, that neat lighting, that cool carpet (the first generation Next): it was Conran Design. As George Davies put it, 'I had to persuade people it would be a false economy to hang onto Kendalls' brown carpets when the Next colour scheme was going to be grey. Terence Conran's influence was… a significant force for good…' Next brought the Design-educated London Look *everywhere.*

When Davies launched the first seven Next branches in February 1982, the takings on day one were two and a half times estimates. And it went on from there. By August 1983, Hepworths, the controlling group, announced that profits had more than doubled from two years earlier, going from £4 million in 1981, to £8.6 million. Once Next for Men was launched in 1984, profits went up again, to £13.6 million.

At the same time, the legend of the Next Corporate Culture was growing. It was said to be like the Moonies: once you worked for Next, you were never the same again – you dedicated yourself to the spread of the Design Attitude, to new ways of thinking, to That Look. Everyone had a uniform allowance so that they could wear the company product, look nice, promote the goods, feel part of the family: 'The uniform allowance was like a Christmas prezzie.' And then, as at least one staffer put it, 'When you spoke to friends about Next, you didn't feel ashamed that you worked in a shop.' And you immersed yourself in the grand homage to George Davies ('George is coming!' you would whisper, when George was about to helicopter out of the heavens onto your branch of the Church of Next). You loved George and the business more than anything else, especially with all the merit awards flying around (trips on the QE2, two weeks in Mauritius, an XR3i Cabriolet – *Yes!*) and what with one thing and another, you became an evangelist.

That was really the golden thread of retailing and buying and consumerism in those happy years – evangelism. Because that's what the glossies and the colour supplements and the high-tone ads and the soft journalists and the conviction merchandisers – Conran, Davies – were doing: they were preaching the gospel to a heathen nation; they were bringing Taste and style and the lust for quality to a nation who had put up with poor taste and deadbeat quality for too long. Next went forth and brought delicious, nice, good taste, *middle-class* sensibilities to all corners of the kingdom. In time, every high street would have one of George's temples in it and no one would have to feel dowdy or hard-done-by or unable to dress the part. Before this time, chainstore ties were almost invariably made of polyester; afterwards, they were almost invariably made of silk.

Retail Design And The Selling Machine

Never forget the look of the shop, in all this. Never forget the cool, sub-trad, guaranteed-the-same-wherever-you-went look of the first Next shops. The philosophy behind the clothes and the philosophy behind the look of the shop were all part of the same thing. And, happy getters and spenders that we were, we had amazing levels of taste formed just from that first encounter with the outside/inside of a Next shop. As

Rodney Fitch put it, back in 1985, 'There was a time when it wasn't seen as necessary to use design to sell. But not any more.'

He should have known, of course, since Fitch, a former Conran lieutenant, along with Conran, was one of the doyens of store design. Fitch got everywhere, from Dorothy Perkins to Burton to Boots to Ravel. In fact, his Dorothy Perkins re-make at the beginning of the eighties, looks exactly like the kind of thing Next was getting away from: chrome fittings, industrial helpings of metal racks all sporting miles of identical, segregated fashion garments, whacky lighting, shamelessly prominent Perspex.

But by 1985, Fitch & Co. had knocked out Wimpy hamburgers and Terminal 4 at Heathrow, and was ready to make over the biggest and drabbest name in the High Street: Woolworths. Only now, he was working with soft, nostalgic, Deco-ish shapes (Woolworths *heritage*, as it might be) and bare timber on the floors. Bare timber was critical, as it turned out: 'It's got a certain nostalgic

These little things, these microcosms of the personality… when the money rage was at its height, you could spend *big* – the house, the car, the intense long-haul holiday experience – or you could spend *small* and surround yourself with tiny daily reminders of your power to discriminate.

appeal.' As did Woolies' 8 million square feet of floor space. And then it was on and up, to the Midland Bank, Thomas Cook, Dillons' bookshop… Once, designers in London amounted to Conran plus a handful of guys in suede brothel-creepers. Now, there were Conran, Fitch and hundreds of others, knocking on the doors of Burtons and Debenhams and the British Airports Authority, looking to carry on the work of evangelizing the shop floor. Environmental design was hot, the new secret weapon for marketing directors.

Maybe it went too far, of course. Not in the Next/Fitch Brave New World of Retail Design, which was usually populist, always with its feet on the ground, but out on the edge, where the UK's sudden infatuation with this new luxury (the luxury of educated senses) started to look just a trifle unwholesome at times. This was when certain people began to get terribly exercised about small things like Braun electric razors and alarm clocks (which had to be so intensely matt black it was sinful). This was when people in the know started talking about Phillipe Starck and Aldo Rossi and Richard Tapper. This was when it became possible to take, some would say, an excessive interest in a Phillipe Starck-designed lemon squeezer, which looked the absolute business, but was marginally worse at squeezing lemons than the old, round, unbreakable glass thing from mum's kitchen, since the Starck item had no way of separating out the pips. This was when some people apparently made a conscious decision to buy themselves a designer kettle – a kettle, used for boiling water – for £70. Not only that, not only a £70 designer kettle, but a non-electric kettle which burnt your fingers when you used it.

Now, this was decadence, this was the same kind of degeneracy which had people turning into fetishists over Porsches and Apple computers and Le Corbusier chairs and mineral water in blue bottles and desk lamps with microscopic 12-volt halogen bulbs that blinded you when you tried to use them. This was the cult end of the evangelical movement. Twenty-five years earlier, the people who were besotted with Braun would have been thrilling themselves with Swedish polished wooden salad bowls or sofa cubes; but in the eighties, when there was so much more to spend and so much to spend it on, the taste cultists became oddly ubiquitous. A few especially resistant British types, lone rearguarders, held these design practices up as tokens of madness, of European nastiness, of phoney values. But they weren't. They were a necessary evil. They were just part of an amazingly accelerated process of learning. You know what auto-didacts are like: they have to tell everyone what they've just learnt…

The Chicken Kiev Revolution

And then Marks & Spencer got in on the taste education business. Of all retailers: M & S, that byword for conservatism, for middle-England caution, had decided to teach us how to eat.

Of course, Sainsbury's and Tesco had been teaching us for a while, now, slowly bringing on the interesting lettuces and curiously-shaped pastas which we now regard as our birthright. There was also the sudden early-eighties rise of the Serious Wine

Archetypal ambience: the Smallbone kitchen, a mass of traditional joinery in painted finishes, spiritual home to the entire nation by 1986, moves suavely into the nineties.

MIKE FAERS

Development Chef, Ross Youngs

KEN GILLIES

Executive, Prepared Foods,
Marks & Spencer

MIKE FAERS

Q How did everything change in the eighties?

A Well I suppose initially food became trendy, if you like, There were a lot of new styles of cuisine that emerged in the eighties which were labelled nouvelle cuisines. There were some good and bad examples as in everything. But I think that made people look at food in a different light. And… obviously as people travel more They think, 'I had this wonderful sun dried tomato product in Italy, I wonder if I can get them over here.' And that's really how it all starts.

Q So are holidays a major thing?

A I think people being able to travel a lot, more frequently and easily, certainly helps to broaden their knowledge of cuisines, yes, without any doubt. And also the up and coming chefs, if you like, the celebrity chefs who emerged during the eighties with the books and the restaurants and the TV series and…

Q Marco and Nico and all those?

A All those, yes. Especially the Roux brothers. They've done a wonderful job for the industry. They've brought it into a high profile industry whereas perhaps before it wasn't seen as that. It's given the industry certainly a lot of, respect if you like.

Q But what's the process whereby all that started going from their house to our house? The idea that the food should be available in a little box.

A Well, certainly people's life styles have changed. It's quite common now for both partners to work… and when [you] get home you might not necessarily want to start cooking a meal. You might want something there that's convenient and quick. That's not to say that food shouldn't be of the highest possible standard [and] that that's really the challenge.

Q What were the different sort of fashions, if you say it was fashion, through the eighties as you remember them, because it must have changed? What was the first big wave?

A I suppose, well nouvelle cuisine itself really is the answer to that. It came upon the restaurant scene in Britain fairly quickly and stayed with us for a good number of years. But I think we've taken the best things out of nouvelle cuisine and perhaps come back a bit from some of the less sensible [things]… I like a decent sized portion but I want it to taste good, I want it to be cooked perfectly and I think that's what really people are after, Good food, good value for money.

Q What else has changed in those ten years?

A Certainly the availability of ingredients is probably the biggest change that's happened. You can now buy, in almost any supermarket, a range of exotic and different ingredients from around the world that you couldn't ten years ago.

KEN GILLIES

Q **Is that by any chance a chicken Kiev would you say?**

A Indeed it is, it's one of the pioneers of convenience food. It was a product that we think established credibility for prepared foods and helped shape and change eating habits in the eighties.

Q **How did it all start?**

A It was remarkably simple. Our chairman at that time visited this very factory almost fifteen years ago and ate this product, and thought it was so wonderful that we just had to have it as part of our product offer. It... established a recipe dish that was difficult to make in the home to a quality level that was as good as you could get in any restaurant but at an affordable price.

Q **What were you aiming to do with prepared foods in the eighties. What was the big idea?**

A The idea was to provide the customer with total convenience, to take away some of the fairly difficult culinary activities that go on in the kitchen and make it as simple as possible for the customer to eat quality products that she may have been used to eating, whether on holidays abroad, or in restaurants, or indeed read about it in the media, or heard about it on television.

Q **What happened next?**

A We then began to get a bit more adventurous and I think the customer was becoming more demanding and more adventurous as well. As we moved from traditionally British fare into Italian foods... we developed a range of, again fairly recognizable [dishes]: the lasagnes, the bologneses, the cannellonis. And, again, I think that height-ened and created an expectation of customers that we would try, even more adventurous and difficult things in the future.

Q **And what followed the Italian food?**

A Well, during the eighties we were seeing a huge development in Chinese restaurants, Indian restaurants. They were appearing in most towns and, again, people felt confident eating those foods. So we started introducing ranges of Chinese foods and, again, our approach was relatively simple. We... established a relationship with Ken Lo, the famous restaurateur, and working closely in conjunction with him, with our suppliers, with our chefs in Baker Street, we established a range of Chinese foods. Our approach to Indian was very similar.

Q **And who was doing the pushing all the time? Was it you saying, 'Well take a risk, push out the envelope,' or was it customers saying we want more and more and more?**

A I think it was a bit of both. I think out aspirations and visions were being heightened all the time. We were challenging ourselves to try and replicate as best we could what our customers were enjoying when they were out at restaurants or at dinners.

Q **Now you're food barmy?**

A I'm certainly passionate about my food, I certainly enjoy good food, and I find it a challenge to constantly keep pace with the fashion of food. And it is constantly changing. We've seen the development of classic dishes to Italian dishes to Indian dishes and Chinese. I'm sure there's much more round the corner.

While George Davies took our wardrobes apart and rebuilt them in his own image, Marks & Spencer brought out the concept of chill-cook, ready-made real things which made the culinary world we'd grown up with seem hopelessly dumb. Pre-prepared dishes became instruments of social change…

Shop – either in the form of Oddbins, or for the real men about town, discount wine warehouses, like the Majestic chain. But what made the M & S manoeuvre so startling was the firm's insistence on running a very *limited*, very high quality line of convenience foods; and pursuing the idea with complete conviction. It seemed so alien at first. Here was M & S, the home of the fawn cardie, getting into these scrupulously dressed and packaged fruit and vegetables, these wine recommendations, these Belgian chocolates, these complex ready-made meals, designed to go through the microwave (the lazy chef's equivalent of the mobile 'phone) and emerge perfect the other side – this was luxury food. This was dinner party food you could (and did) bang on the plate for your friends and acquaintances and then sit there, garnering praise. In fact, you got the praise even when you told them the stuff had come from Marks. Everyone thought, how clever.

How did it happen? Because you have to bear in mind that this was a time when you couldn't move for people junking their eating habits of ten years earlier – which, in the main, meant getting shot of those heinous seventies convenience foods and replacing them with something fresh, tasty and real. There was this yearning for deep quality, bolstered up by all sorts of new cultural considerations. Food was becoming more and more clearly a mark of cultural maturity: it always had been, of course, ever since the days when your ability to handle a lobster without harming yourself was the mark of the couth classes; and when a broad knowledge of French wines marked you down as a Bohemian.

But now Britons travelled a lot to longer-haul, more interesting places – taxi drivers to Miami, small traders to Barbados – where the food was altogether something else; they tried at least to get to grips with some more demanding wine than Blue Nun (Le Piat D'or fitted the bill very nicely for those who found the Liebfraumilch just a trifle candyfloss, but weren't ready for a full *premier cru*). Snob food, like snob drinks, took a sudden leap forward. Like so many things we thought we couldn't do, we found we could cope with the stuff. Kitchens, utilitarian until the seventies, started to become the social and cultural centres of houses. Quite modest middle-class smallholders spent fortunes on Smallbone joinery (£30 000 was not uncommon) and Poggenpohl fixtures and Miele dishwashers and AEG fan ovens and glass jars from the Conran shop and strainers from the Reject Shop and Le Creuset saucepans.

But it all had to be paid for with longer hours and moonlighting. So, however much you wanted the squid cooked in its own ink plus fresh *penne*, you didn't really have the time to get down to it. Friday nights and weekends, maybe, but otherwise, it was a bit of a strain. Instead, we ate out an awful lot more and got to like it. The *Good Food Guide* (which had actually been going for thirty years) started to appear in the most unlikely sitting-rooms. We could afford it, for heaven's sake. So many restaurants were wired for credit cards these days, it seemed pointless not to. And yet, at the same time, it was kind of nice to eat in….

So M & S squared this particular circle. They gave it to us fresh and instant. They re-invented convenience food and banished the nightmares of the preceding decades. Even things like the *vegetables* – the carrots and potatoes and general foot-soldiers of the kitchen – were sorted and washed and graded and 'batoned' so that you didn't really have to do anything with them except plunge them into boiling water. At the same time, you could get your ready-made Chicken Kiev and either microwave it in between telephone calls, or cook it properly in an oven if you had someone coming round. There was a time when Chicken Kiev was luxury food, something you only got in restaurants, and in the seventies, only restaurants in the really big cities, at that.

Now Kievs were as handy as a tin of beans. By the end of the eighties they came in multiples so you could give them to your children. They were in some ways the equivalent of the silk tie, going from utter rarity to indispensible commonplace in five years flat. Even things like apples (nature's very own convenience snack) were brought to a new level of sophistication, being chosen by the team at M & S for their looks as well as their taste and texture, before being lovingly packaged in little shining quartets, like Fabergé eggs.

And to show how serious, how uncompromising they were, M & S even let the shelves empty themselves. After all the supermarkets had taught us about our right to expect whatever we wanted, whenever we wanted it, M & S used their empty shelves (that desperate hunt for the last packet of green beans after 5.30 pm…) as a marketing device. It said: we care so much about the absolute daily freshness of our produce that we will only put the stuff out at a time that's right for the food. It was like some Continental marketplace just before closing time. And – just like a swank foodstore in Milan or Bordeaux – they charged rather more than one was used to paying, because, of course, it was worth it. The whole experience was *that real.*

The upshot was that by 1987, Marks & Spencer had food sales alone of £1.5 billion and were talking about opening their first-ever food-only store. They already had some six shops in London selling *mostly* food, plus a few socks and staples. But this was a sign of something new, the tangible recognition of the fact that Marks had become one of the country's top ten food retailers – and much the most expensive.

Was this evangelism, though? Was it like the George Davies Mission? Only up to a point: the real propagandizing was being done by a mixture of the soft-feature press, the glossies and Sainsbury's and Tesco. They were the ones prompting us towards rocket, or espresso coffee, or woodcock in Balsamic vinegar. M & S, typically, weren't walking on the wild side (you only had to look at their early own-brand French wines to see how unfrightening they were). They made what you knew and already wanted – from holidays and restaurants – better and more accessible than it had ever been.

Our Gorgeous Life

Taste, luxury, evangelism… they didn't stop at the High Street, mark you. This business of quality, of improvement in the tangible realities of your life, went in other directions. One the one hand, we wanted better things around us, better threads on our backs, better food on our plates, but we also wanted to be better human beings. We wanted to be better lovers, stronger atheletes, improved specimens of the race. Eighties' good food is a kissing cousin of the eighties' diet programmes, of the obsession with shape, of that explosion of interest in changing the way we looked and putting something bigger and swankier in its place. You've bought the externals: now buy yourself something smart to shove inside them.

Those maniacs in the City who were putting in fourteen-hour days at the bleeping terminals wanted it to be known that they were supermen, not just because of the money they packed, or the hours they worked, but because they staggered off in their lunch breaks to fight it out in a contest of wills with a Nautilus machine – and then staggered off after work to down a bottle of the white Burgundy they'd known nothing about twelve months earlier. Those TV shows – *Dallas, Dynasty* – churned the whole lot together: clothes, food, the art of the body, *things*, frenzied self-improvement, the unending quest of the Self, nothing but The Best.

Around about this time, Sly Stallone was really milking the Rocky character and touching the spirit of the age (*Rocky III*, in 1982, with the 'Eye Of The Tiger' theme tune; followed by *IV* in 1985, in which Rocky – out of the ring and polishing a Ferrari – has to rebuild himself for a geopolitical showdown with a Russian heavy by chopping logs, doing chin-ups in a wood cabin, etc.) with an almost industrial undertow of self-perfection, of *total* betterment. And there was Schwarzenegger, slowly marking out his unique patch of cultural territory, but first of all becoming an icon simply as a product of the most determined self-invention: the body, the attitude, the money that sprang from it... almost as if he'd *bought the lot*....

That's what it was all for, all the money, all the hot credit and the Good Things. Unlike earlier cash-rich moments in history – the late fifties, the credit boom of the early seventies – when consumption was a way of doing something about your place in society, getting your share, but *this* was all about something altogether more transcendant, the altar of the ego. This time we were looking for a different kind of result, as if we'd been away for a long time, or in prison; we were doing this for *ourselves*.

P R O P E R T Y

Well, there were parties and there were parties. And the biggest, the best, the longest-running, the party with most goodies on offer and the most amusing things to fool around with, was the Property Party. It ran from 1979 all the way to 1988, with guests arriving all the time. In fact, you couldn't separate the Property from the Party: there were parties to launch prestige developments in Kensington; there were parties to celebrate your friends' latest house move (only *slightly* speculative: Salford Docks are already going up); there were parties to announce the first wholly-finished refurbishment in a tea warehouse overlooking Shad Thames, with a healthy secondary market in invitations starting up ten days beforehand....

The Home-Loan Hitlers

Think back a long way, a very long way. Think back to what house-buying was like, some time in the 1970s. In those days, about the only people who would lend you the cash to buy your studio flat or your four-bedroomed effort perilously close to Whalley Range were members of your family or a building society. And that was it. Building societies, those strange, Victorian mutuals of the High Street, had an effective monopoly on housing finance. The clearing banks were stuffed into something called the Corset, which basically made it not worth their while getting into the mortgage market. The American loan specialists weren't around. Money for mortgages seemed in costively short supply and your choice of loanster was limited to competing shades of grey. Remember the mortgage queue? This was where it started.

If you were really serious and wanted the money to buy somewhere, it was like being received into the Roman Catholic Church, only more arduous. First, you had to start saving with your Local & Friendly Society from about the age of four to demonstrate your credentials as a long-term person. Then you had to come out and actually ask for the cash, which was a humiliating experience because building society managers were apt to treat you as something between a reformed borstal boy and a mental defective. And then you had to prove that you could pay back the 50 or 60 per cent of the property's value that the society was grudgingly thinking of letting you have, thanks to a good job, a responsible attitude towards debt, and a clean parting down the middle of your head. The loan itself would be, at most, two and a half times your earnings.

Worst of all, perhaps, was the invariability of the whole procedure. The societies had been running their businesses for forty years as a cartel, with nothing to choose between them on interest rates or earnings multiples or restrictions or provisos. It didn't matter whose glumly-varnished doors you pushed open: on the other side was the same man in a pair of Peter Sellers specs, with the same Building Societies' Association rule book on the shelf behind him dictating precisely the same routine.

I'm liquid! Buy me! Agency options go boomtime; and everyone has a property portfolio.

As a consequence, partly, of all this, we were talking four beds in a nice bourgeois suburb almost anywhere for £30 000, back in 1978.

Rolling In It: The Money Supply Mania

But in 1979 the new government quietly got shot of the restrictions on building society lending and, in 1980, it removed the Corset, which let the banks get in on the act (by 1982, they had 30 per cent of the new mortgage business). A year or so later, the building societies' cartel collapsed, and a couple of years after that, the American moneylenders appeared on the scene, eager to channel funds into the UK market. Strangely enough, the societies didn't even object. The demand for property money was so huge that they were just grateful to be out of the spotlight and away from everyone's gripes about tight-arsed home loan Hitlers. They just sat back like everyone else and watched as the cash tap wasn't just turned on, but unbolted from the wall and thrown into a skip. From nowhere, from out of a clear blue sky, we found ourselves up to our ears in ready money.

Nor was this your usual British a-bit-here-a-bit-there dispensation. These were vast sums, bizarre quantities of money in comparison with what had gone before. The lenders found themselves dishing out over 100 per cent of the value of the property on occasions (after all, you had to have a little something left over to spend on the Colefax & Fowler) and four times your earnings. Did it matter that the loans were usually based on the applicant's own assessment of his or her earning power? Did it matter that the hopeful chancer could barely write his own name? Not a jot – because this money was going into property, and property was better than Krugerrands, it was better than Gilts, it was better than De Koonings or Facel-Vegas, it was the staff of life to the lenders and usurers, because bricks and mortar, so they had come to believe, would always hold their value (but more likely go up – vertically). All this liberated us to go after the Good Stuff, it gave us the feeling that the money was ours by right, that it wasn't really borrowing at all because, if we 'owned' – i.e. were buying – a house we were rich anyway. We had 'capital' or a major asset or, to use the eighties word 'equity'. The startling appreciation in domestic property values when the majority were owner-occupiers underwrote some *very* bold spending.

Seeing The Potential

So the crucial money was there. But where were the houses? Now, this is where it starts to sound a bit more familiar, because one the great blessings of the eighties Property Party was that it woke everyone up to the fact that the houses were actually everywhere and that everywhere is redeemable. Seeing the potential became the mark of a man.

Another mark of the old days, the building society years: you couldn't borrow on a place they didn't like. Money was tied up in the sensible suburbs, the good area places in the centre of town, the reliable countryside, the unthreatening Barratt Homes. Where you could live was about as well defined and rationed as the kind of money you could expect to spend on it. Building society London, for instance, was out in Finchley, or Hampstead Garden Suburb, or St John's Wood, or (heaven help us) Croydon and Carshalton. It was typified by a certain architectural sensibility: repro vernacular, Norman Shaw as seen through a Wates balance-sheet, Edwardian timber and tile (provided it was in good repair) all the way through to the Suntrap houses sprawling out to the outer suburbs of any major city. It was a world in which people were still having difficulty making up their minds over any modernist box and where somewhere different meant Chelsea.

But once the money was there, the property market did a typically eighties' *volte-face*. Having been slow and steady for a longish while, it suddenly went berserk: raging over-consumption started to shift the goods at an incredible rate. From mortgage queues, we went in the space of two years to property queues. Instead of lending only on the solid stuff, the mainstream suburb stuff, building societies and banks were practically falling over themselves to lend on just about anything with windows and a door. Property of any kind became intensely desirable and it wasn't long before *gazumping* (etymology unknown) hit the streets and large numbers of people found themselves dazed and reeling after a robust encounter with an estate agent. This wasn't helped in the south east, incidentally, by the swelling ranks of City boys and girls, who, in the years leading up to Big Bang were finding themselves amalgamated, head-hunted and handcuffed at vastly inflated fees, and who then decided that it was time to settle down in a little place of their own. Nor was it helped by an influx of American money people, also after a piece of deregulated City action, but packing even more immense – let's be honest, transatlantic – wage slips. In these fraught circumstances, the good news was that even if you couldn't buy a £175 000 town house straight out of your own pocket (which a surprising number of these Parallel Universe people found they could), at least the opportunities to borrow the cash were superabundant.

Go South, Young Banker

So the money chased the properties – starting, of course, in London – and before you knew it, the best parts were going off the top of the graph and even the newly gentrified areas (which a decade before were only just beginning to look *plausible*, let alone *indispensible*) were outpricing themselves. And then the great migration south of London began in earnest. Clapham started to evolve into The Banker's Dormitory. Around the country a range of Claphams in every major city would follow.

Hard to recall, it's true, but Clapham and Battersea, over the river in south London, used to be a bit of a joke. What did we have here before the eighties glamorised it? We had the Battersea Power Station, Giles Gilbert Scott's upturned coffee table, finally switched off in 1983 and left pointing aimlessly at the south London sky. We had Lavender Hill, where Stanley Holloway and Alec Guinness did their stuff for the 1951 Ealing Comedy *The Lavender Hill Mob* (the air turns brown – the colour of post-war office furniture – just thinking about it). And we had Clapham Common, synonymous with teddy boys, flashers, low voltage violence and bus exhausts. Goods and services at the time? A launderette or two, a newsagent's, a couple of caffs in the traditional mode and the odd belligerent greengrocer.

And yet, within about eighteen months, this corner of south-west London became so stiff with young investment analysts, bond dealers and would-be partners of the heavy law firms (Linklater's, Freshfields, Slaughter & May; it was like the Oxford University appointments committee down there) that if the City itself had disappeared into a hole in the ground one night, half of its business could have been carried on in SW11. Better yet, this otherwise limited mix was invigorated (in the fullness of time) by cultural heavy-hitters like Paul Theroux, Snoo Wilson, Ian McEwan and Howard Jacobson: cash, saucily rubbing up against the Sunday supplements. Even the food perked up, as the legendary Tea Time eaterie got into its stride, followed by the Bianco Verdi and the Inebriated Newt for the children of the City, with Harveys (no less) a quick cab ride away on the edge of Wandsworth Common. *Why?*

Post-Modern Means 1910

Because it was Old Hat, for a start. That was one of the really beautiful things about the early eighties: it was a time when we could forget all the dreadful foreign nonsense about Modernism and Mies and Gropius and stop having to admire Scandanavian kitchen designs. Instead, we got back to where we felt we belonged – which, as it turned out, was somewhere post about 1870, with large panelled doors, an awful lot of stairs, dado rails wherever you looked, and a huge 'period feature' fireplace. Suddenly, it was all right again. We didn't have to *try* any more. It was enough just to gaze at our Delft-pattern fire surrounds.

Just as beautiful in many ways, was the fact that we also had an awful lot of very new, hard currency. Now that *was* heaven – not only was it permissible to indulge this degenerate passion for the past (every Englishman's birthright) but also we finally had the resources to do it properly. *Real* (how could we have ever kidded ourselves otherwise?) was *big* and *reasonably old* and *not unreasonably priced* and surrounded by *similar-looking stuff*, just to reassure us that, however much it felt like wandering off into the wastes of Mongolia, we were actually neighbours to thousands of like-minded people. And it happened everywhere, this expansive Forsyteian . No merchant's home in Glasgow was safe.

So it was on with the Dulux primrose yellow for the drawing-room (with maybe a rakish Adam red for the stairs and hall) and in with the Neff fan oven and down with some fitted coir matting on account of the dog.

And there was a new sense of scale down here – not just in the broad expanses of those nineteenth-century bourgeois minor suburbs and their green spaces, but in the sheer size of those houses. It was size as well as period tastiness which helped to make the experience so lovely. From now on, you could work on the Jaguar privatization and live like a King. Just think, four bedrooms! (Some had six.) Your parents had to wait decades to get four bedrooms! And how much wall and floor space there was for you to express all that *taste* which had been building up ever since you left university! At last: a canvas big enough on which to portray the fascinating life you wanted to lead!

But there was yet another benefit. This sudden rediscovery of a whole tract of London led to the rediscovery of other tracts of London. Just as Fulham decamped to Clapham and Battersea, so Islington decamped to Hackney and Bethnal Green. St John's Wood found out that Kilburn, Shepherd's Bush and Hammersmith could also support human life. And Hampstead shifted its weight in the direction of Camden Town and Kentish Town and found it, if not good, at least a lot better than it had at first appeared.

Naming The Party

And this in turn gave us more joy of London villages. Where you live necessarily speaks volumes about you, and in London the game of London Villages (Hampstead v. Camden v. Notting Hill v. Barnes, and so on) has always been one of the great metropolitan pastimes. Only now, the game was abruptly bigger, more complicated and an awful lot more fun. South London, got carved up into South Chelsea (aka Battersea), while Clapham was called *Claam, ha, ha,* by its inmates. Stockwell and Streatham (isn't that just taking things a bit too far?) turned into St Ockwell and St Reatham. Kilburn hid behind the assumed double barrel of West Hampstead (no, it *is,* really), while Hackney made a big thing out of London Fields. Taxi drivers didn't know what had hit them – two in the morning, a constant stream of well-dressed drunks heading up and down the Latchmere Road like the support staff of an advancing army… But even deeper than that, were the villages-within-villages. You might have been in Clapham, but were you Battersea Rise Clapham, Abbeville Road (aka Abbeville Village) Clapham, or were you North Side/Pavement Clapham? Were you Barons Court Hammersmith, Goldhawk Road Hammersmith, or Turnham Green Hammersmith? For God's sake, let's not beat about the bush: *which tube station did you use?* And provincials, who started deriding the angels-on-a-pinhead geographical nuances of London in the early eighties, found themselves plunging in before the decade was out.

It was a hoot, partly because it pandered so deliciously to the old vice of social grading and sorting; but also because – strangest of all to the English notion of continuity – it told us over and over again, that we could go out and claim new parts of the world, we could put those old, big, buildings back to work, we could explore, experiment. London effectively doubled in size: everywhere was redeemable. The historic village experiment was profoundly radical and deregulated.

NY On Thames and the Boho Warehouse Look

And nowhere was more incredibly *redeemed* than Docklands: the eighties in two square miles. Step one: you close down, between 1967 and 1980, London's vast, unworkable inner commercial docks and leave the business to Tilbury, way out in the Thames estuary. Step two: along comes a visionary – in this case, someone like the South African expat Rae Hoffenberg, who falls in love with the 'sky and the river and the birds and the light and the sunrise and the sunsets' in the mid-seventies, and immediately begins a war of attrition with the corporate entities responsible for Docklands. This is the opening gambit in her attempt to become the first person to realise their latent appeal as a stunning place to live in. Step three: in 1981, the then Environment Secretary, Michael Heseltine, launches the London Docklands Development Corporation, following this up a year later with £22 million of sweeteners and incentives for anyone and everyone who wants to take part. Step four: step back and wait as the rest of the world raises unimaginable sums of money just to *be there*.

Of course, *Docklands* means anything and everything from the News International bunker at Wapping, to the Limehouse Basin, to the jolly little execs' tenements around South Quay Plaza. But first and foremost, the word was associated with the Rae Hoffenberg vision, those spectacular lumps of meaty industrial archaeology, warehouses, magically transformed into fabulous Boho dens for City tyros – that was Docklands. And it was transfixing for two very good reasons.

First, it was the apotheosis of London's new redeemability. While it was one thing to reclaim North Clapham, with its large, sensible houses and its tolerable infrastructure, it was an imaginative leap of a different order to reclaim a load of huge, rotting tea and coffee warehouses in a part of London which was not only virtually off the map (especially since London has been shifting west, not east, ever since the Romans left) but quite impossible to get to. This was striking out with a vengeance – this was boldness, confidence, can-do, the excitement of discovering *terra nova* in a way which no one could remember experiencing before. It was, simply, inspirational: if we could do this, turn the map of London inside-out, then nothing was impossible.

And secondly, it conjured up a little bit of New York – quite magically – out of the dark Thames mud. Now, the US/GB relationship had been warming up ever since Reagan and Thatcher began their trysting at the end of the seventies. Both governments were mouthing the same gung-ho individualist rhetoric; both governments were busily tipping money into the middle-class voter's pockets while telling him or her that it was cool to be a me-first materialist. In London itself, American money was sloshing around courtesy of the big Stateside institutions which were buying into Europe and the UK money markets; and American culture was in the ascendant – great images reeking of strength, wealth, self-transformation and self-reliance were everywhere – Tina Turner, Rocky, the Boss, *Dallas*; New York and Los Angeles were, more than ever, the places to have just come back from.

Awaiting redemption: mud, bricks and a million rats.

Above Don't you just *wish*? the Big Window, the essential architectural shape of the age, streaming with light from the dirty old river — a converted apartment on the Thames.

INTERVIEW

RAE HOFFENBERG

Designer and developer

Q Tell me how you came to find this part of the world?

A Well, it's quite a long story... I was living in the West End. It was the early seventies and I was having a difficult time trying to organise my life and restore the house I was living in. I had great difficulties with the bureaucrats... I just felt so constricted in the West End I wanted to get out. I wanted to see the sky.

Q You've got a lot of sky here.

A Yes I have and I love it. I absolutely love it... I started to drive along the river with a ribbon of buildings alongside it.

Q But something caught your imagination.

A Well, I stopped the car and wandered down some steps. You could see the water from the steps and it was so beautiful – I didn't see the dereliction. What I saw was water, I saw the sky and the odd passing boat. I decided to live there and I persuaded my husband that he would love it.

Q Was it a house or what?

A There were a group of derelict warehouses, a terrace of nineteenth century warehouses totally abandoned. The entire river was abandoned... a derelict wasteland. I fell in love and said this is where I want to live. So I bought it. It took three years to get planning permission. I had no idea I was going to have such difficulty. But

that was what it was like. The dead hand of government was everywhere. I was sent from Tower Hamlets to the GLC and back again. The GLC were the strategic planners. They didn't know what they wanted to do with the area and neither did Tower Hamlets.

Q So you found yourself becoming a developer – how did that happen?

A Once I decided that I was going to live in this old wharf and had all these other derelict wharfs around me, I was terrified that anyone should come along and pull them down and build high-rise towers. I created a precedent by eventually getting planning permission, which immediately opened the floodgates. This [was] the late seventies... I was very nervous about the lovely old buildings... so I decided that I would try and acquire them. But I didn't have to do that, they were offered to me.

Q You make it sound like rescuing.

A Yes, yes, they would've been pulled down if I hadn't saved them, as many in the Docklands have been... It was just a great battle with the bureaucrats... and then suddenly everything changed. There was this brand new awakening - Margaret Thatcher appeared on the scene with her lieutenants and it was the golden age of opportunity.

So when it turned out that we actually had a piece of Americana right on the doorstep – the great Boho loft, with its bare brick, its beams and its huge, daylight-charged windows – it was almost too good to be true. Did it matter that those Boho lofts actually needed a hell of a lot of treatment before they were light enough, comfortable enough and safe enough to use – that they needed to be practically rebuilt? Did it matter than many of them became a baffling mish-mash of styles, of fake, repro, anachronistic and original? It didn't matter a bit: they still looked great.

Remember the ad for the Halifax Building Society (ironically enough) in which the funky bachelor wakes up in his Cinnamon Street conversion on a Sunday morning, no milk, no ready cash, a quick trip from the warehouse front door to the hole-in-the-wall and he's sorted? That was the dream, that was *it*, made flesh. Being an ad of course, it was already slightly behind the times when it first appeared, but it caught perfectly the mood of the moment about five years earlier. Now, put that dream together with the new cash-rich sense of mobility and freedom which sharp bourgeois Londoners were already starting to think of as theirs for evermore, and you have the most highly-charged set of circumstances since the day the Beatles brought out 'Revolver'. At least one flat in Docklands went for £43 000 in 1979; and re-sold, untouched, in 1989, for £167 500. The cost of land alone went up from £36 500 an acre to £150 000 an acre in boring Beckton; while in the sexier Surrey Docks, it was up to £400 000 an acre by the mid-eighties.

The B-Movie Lifestyle Deal

Needless to say, there weren't enough pure Boho warehouse conversions to go round (and besides, not everyone wanted to live in a flat the size and shape of a football pitch, with no internal walls and a lot of cast-iron to catch your forehead on), but this didn't dampen the mood. Another eighties' inversion: *new* would *do*, provided it came with flair and a breezy, post-modern sensibility. It was cool: people who could cope with the look called the whole thing B-Movie Architecture, just to show how clever and culturally complex the experience was.

But who was doing B-Movie Architecture in those days? Enter Piers Gough, the architect who decided to make an 'heroic statement about being high rise'. And what did this heroic statement turn out to be? The Isle of Dogs' very own Cascades: the tower block deconstructed, tipped on its side, stepped like a broken waterfall, perched

Can it be real? When Cascades opened up, it was like a weird shipment from Los Angeles abruptly arriving Thames-side. Film set as lifestyle.

The Circle: blue walls, jagged profiles, Piers Gough surrealism, Bel-Air aspirations, the property dream on the cusp of a nightmare.

FRED PARKIN

A former tenant who bought his council house

Q Fred, tell me a bit about what you did to the front of the house?

A Well, John next door was the first one to buy his house along here. And he put the porch on, which was nice. And when I bought my house, I thought, well, to make it sort of come in line with his, I would build a porch. But then, when I looked at the living room, I thought, well, while I'm building a porch I might as well go straight across and extend the living room area. So...

Q And you'd have a couple of feet right the way through.

A Right the way through, yes. So I put a metre right across the front of the house... We'd liked to have come out further, but then we'd have had no front garden.

Q And when you were thinking about it, what did you want it to end up looking like?

A We drove about, round Dagenham and Barking and different places, to see how people had done their houses and I got a picture of how we'd like ours done which is the leaded lights, the bay windows and a bit of pebbledash.

Q Yes. And then a new door?

A A new door.

Q It's got fourteen rooms now.

A [Laughs] Yes.

[Inside]

Q Oh it's all beams.

A Yes.

Q Did you do this?

A Yes, this is all my own work here.

Q What were you aiming for, what was the look here?

A Well, it was virtually basic when we first moved in only wallpaper and I thought to myself, well we'll make it look like a little bit olde worlde which was the in-thing just then.

Q And it goes with the leaded lights.

A That's right. The house is worth more in scrap, I think, that it is in bricks, with all this lead.

Q How did you feel when you first heard about the right to buy?

A Oh, I think it was the greatest thing that the ordinary working person had offered to him. I bought this house for £10 000. After a couple of years they valued it at £68 000.

Q And was that when you started doing all of these things to the house?

A Oh yes. Once we went in to buy it, I thought, well now I can get stuck in.

Q Now, looking back from the nineties, how do you feel about the property boom?

A Me? I think it was hyped up so much. Over-priced. Well over-priced right the way through.

Q Do your friends feel the same way as you do, are they glad they bought?

A Oh yes, definitely. Because your mortgage has got to be a lot cheaper than rent is. I think it's a great thing. And we're landowners.

on the banks of the Thames and equipped, handily enough, with a swimming pool, a sauna, tennis courts and twenty-four-hour staffing for all those boys and girls who were too busy to pick up the mail, hoover the carpets or even get home at nights. Sounds like another world – sounds like a Manhattan stage on which to act out your life. And what do you know, but queues were forming within twenty-four hours of the first showing of the model? The place hadn't even been *built* and you had people who took no more than ten minutes to make up their minds and then *bang* – they'd put down the £25 000 deposit and come back a year later to see what it was they'd bought. That was how far we'd come since 1979: design a life, be bold, take a flyer, *be the dream.*

Such a brilliant concept was this, that it drifted clean out of Docklands and transplanted itself further down the river, down by the gas works at Sands End, in extremely deep Fulham. Now, Fulham hadn't had any architectural concepts for a long while – not since the Hurlingham Club, some might argue – but such was the mood of iconoclasm at the time, it suddenly seemed entirely right that SW10 should get its own shining new temple to the Spirit of the Age.

Calling itself Chelsea Harbour, this 'prestige development' offered not only sky-high prices (that guarantee of stylish exclusivity) but also the chance to purchase a berth for your Monte-Carlo-style motor yacht in the marina below. So it's a motor yacht on the cold, brown Thames, with the open sea fifty miles away at Southend – *it doesn't matter: you've got it and they haven't. Be the dream.* The gates would open at 8.30 in the morning and by 9.30, the clever young estate agency boys would have sold 50 reservations, working from a caravan on the site. Mandatory reading material for the realty boys at the time? Donald Trump's *The Art Of The Deal.*

The Half-Timbered High-Rise

Streatham, the Millwall Docks, high-rise living – everywhere is redeemable. And if you didn't believe it, there was this final proof: in September 1986, Mrs Thatcher turned up like something out of the Brothers Grimm on the doorstep of a house in Forres, in north-east Scotland. In bright sunshine, and to the delight of the *Forres, Elgin & Nairn Gazette,* she presented the owners of this modest dwelling with a certificate to mark the fact that their house was the one millionth council house sale in Britain. Not bad going, not bad going *at all,* when you consider that council tenants had only received the right to buy in October of 1980, under the Housing Act of the same year – making it obligatory for councils to sell their houses to anyone who wanted to buy, provided they'd been tenants for a minimum of three years.

It was another genie out of another bottle. A couple of years of Housing Act delirium (gleefully talked up by the *Sun*, under such headlines as OURS, ALL OURS and COUNCIL HOUSE GIVES JIM A PROFIT OF £164 000) and you realized that the Property Party really was happening all over. It wasn't just the children of the City who were doing it, it was coming up from below – coming at you from all sides. Seriously:

Baronial in Barking. Everything was possible. Light-headed with choice, we struck out in all directions and affirmed every Englishman's right to be a bourgeois anarchist. Cladding *meant* freedom.

a tenant in Hillingdon bought his council bungalow for £83 500 and sold it after a month for £165 000; another in Mottingham splashed out £34 000 for his place, only to have it valued at £85 000 a year later; a parks director in Leeds paid £70 000 for a house subsequently valued at £250 000….

And once they'd bought their own places, the ex-tenants, now just-like-you-and-me freeholders, decided to stamp their personalities on their caves in the time-honoured British freeholder tradition. They knocked through, they built arches, they shoved on porches, they stone-clad, they plumbed in whirlpool baths, they clad (inside and out) with GRP imitation half-timbering for that country pub look, they jammed in fireplaces, cocktail cabinets, patios and bubble-bath carpets. Thirty thousand pounds to buy; £15 000 to get it looking nice – that was the order of the day.

Self-Expression And The Art Of Paper Hanging

There's a common thread, connecting the Clapham missionaries, the Docklands visionaries, the new-build go-getters, the council house jackpot-winners: your home

Victorian hippy millionaires — we could do it if we wanted to. And Jocasta Innes showed us how — by loading up on swags, stage props, Queen Victoria's wallpaper and a credit card.

became your *hobby*. Instead of being that place where you lived and ate and slept, and which was a kind of familiar, faintly shabby life fixture, like an old pullover — it became an arena, a theatre for your creativity, a permanent hobby, a crucible for self-expression. Familiar enough, the old saw about mid-eighties' pub conversations revolving perpetually around the one question, 'How Much Has Your House Gone Up In Value?' But it's nonetheless true: our homes started to occupy the forefront of consciousness in a wholly new way. It didn't matter if you were the type who gave dinner parties where everyone asked That Question, or if your preferred to sit in a freshly-furbished theme pub and talk XR3s. Home became a pastime, an all-consuming interest — either because you were transfixed by the financial ramifications and potentialities which gathered around it like a sulphurous mist; or because you were obsessed with it as a decorative opportunity; or even because, having schlepped all the way to Bethnal Green with your heart in your mouth, you found your were living in a piece of history and it was the first time anything so momentous had ever happened to you… Your home allowed you to *express yourself.*

And there were plenty of people around to help you *express yourself* just as much as your little heart desired. Remember, this was the time when every man's wife, girlfriend or cousin suddenly seemed to be an interior designer. From being the preserve of the David Hickses and the Tricia Guilds, interior design (epitomized by a mass attack of yellow emulsion, blue-and-white pinstriped wallpaper and Nitromorsed dining-room doors) became the nation's playground. If you couldn't do it yourself, you

INTERVIEW

MIN HOGG

Editor, *The World of Interiors*

Q Min, why did top people turn into decormaniacs in the early 1980s?

A Oh, I rather like to think I had something to do with it. I started World of Interiors magazine, but I didn't know at the time it was going to have any influence whatsoever, because what I was interested in doing was showing the readers, if there were going to be any which we didn't know at the start, all kinds of houses that I knew of myself, and which I had been kind of mentally collecting all my life, but that never ever got into magazines. I was always suggesting them on the other magazines where I worked, but the answer was invariably no. So I was rather pleased when I was finally allowed to show them all to the public.

Q Why were the early 1980s right for doing up houses, why not the seventies, why was it then?

A I think it's rather like changes in clothes fashions, there was something in the air which everyone grabbed and it took off in a most amazing way. I couldn't believe it… I wasn't trying to say to people, go out and spend, I was saying, look at these wonderful things, aren't they nice just to look at. Then our influences started to appear. For instance when my magazine World of Interiors had shown crumbling old houses,

stately homes on their last tottering legs that in turn influenced people who bought a crumbling stately home and turned it into a country house hotel. The guests at the country house hotel suddenly, for the first time, found themselves living pseudo lives of being in a stately home which… in turn they took home and tried to re-create in their houses.

Q So it went from you setting the style, to people mugging it up a sort of stage set and thing, I want a tiny version of this at home in Laurels?

A Of course there was another branch, because… there were certainly those people whose idea of decorating was just an even bigger hi-fi and a simple chair, and there are endless houses, most of which I refused to publish, where that was literally the decor. There were no curtains, there was a clean floor, varnished, and then an enormous amount of equipment, and the speakers were instead of the Rembrandt.

Q So hi tech was on another strand of decormania?

A Yes, completely separate.

Q And you could spend lots of money?

A You could spend – the sky was the limit.

Q For you, what are the key icons, the key symbols of 1980s decormania?

A The key symbols. Quite a lot of them are things like the fitted kitchen, the Smallbone kitchen, the floor of fake Provençal tiles in your Mayfair apartment, amazing showers and baths. A lot of money was spent. I think people thought when they sold their house for a vast profit, it would double that profit if they had all those status things as well and I suppose the very rich went and bought a bigger Rembrandt.

Q What effect do you think the country house hotel boom had?

A I think it had a huge effect, because alongside the boon in country houses turned into hotels… another strand of people was opening decorating shops all over England, the big chains all got into it, but also on a higher level, little shops, little decorating shops selling the same merchandise that you could buy in London. After all, all they needed was a pattern book with silk costing a thousand pounds a metre. It didn't cost the shop anything to have it, but it did spread the word and people were getting keener and keener on buying it, doing up their houses non stop.

Q Did decoration become a branded, designery area like fashion?

A Yes, I certainly think it did and there were looks, there was the Colefax and Fowler look that was aped by all the Carolines and Emmas because that was the top… but there were plenty of other looks on the market that if you wanted your friends to know that you'd gone to the top, you would indeed go, for instance, to Czech and Speake to get your bathroom. If you could only afford the soap dish, that was a start, but you could get the whole of it and it would stand out like a sore thumb, everybody would know, who went into your bathroom, how much money you'd spent because you'd been to the top place.

Q How did Interiors promote itself in the launch days in 1981? What did it say?

A It encapsulated what I was trying to do, which was to show people things they'd never, never seen before. Let them through the door of places that they wouldn't otherwise have access [to] and we used the line on posters that were all over the motorways before the launch which said – 'How the other half live' and then, wham, bam, the first issue did indeed do that. And I think people were fascinated to find that the pop star Bryan Ferry lived in this extremely exceedingly grown-up flat when they were expecting him to live somewhere with Mickey Mouse and tinsel town horrors and gold discs. There it was, the miniature stately home in a small studio flat in London. Every element was there, the pediments on the bookcases, the ruched blinds, the coffee table… two kinds of chintz on the curtains, blue and white china. there was even a feature in the same issue on blue and white china. He was right there before we began.

Q Why did the publishers of Interiors think there was market for a big shiny expensive magazine about posh houses?

A Well, the publisher saw a gap which was neither covered by House and Garden, nor covered by the next sort of layer down, like Homes and Gardens. He felt it should be much more international magazine, probably based on one already existing in America. In fact, I didn't fulfil his dreams in that way, but that was certainly what he thought. We found another gap, and so it rolled off in that direction.

could bet that someone down the street would be starting up a little business from the front half of their sitting room (and would be just delighted to pop in and talk curtain materials for half a morning and a small commision.

But if you could do it yourself, then you damn well Did It Yourself, with a little assistance from your new friends at B & Q and Texas. This too, became a sideshow of some importance: by the mid-eighties, DIY had become the second most popular leisure activity after watching TV, according to a survey commissioned by Polycell, those well-known manufacturers of DIY requisites. The DIY market as a whole, grew by 30 per cent between 1983 and 1986, hitting a total value of £3.2 billion in 1987. B & Q alone were taking 23 per cent of all sales by that year.

Actually, B & Q were not just making a profit out of the self-expression craze, they were instrumental in defining the way we thought of ourselves as we went about our labours of creativity. The B & Q warehouse approach said it all: it was big, competent, businesslike, taking care of everything from itty-bitty brass screws to lengths of 5-inch diameter wastepiping to sprigged wallpaper to burglar alarms. And by extension, we too were big, competent and businesslike. We knew we could handle anything from a window lock to a complete re-wiring of the upstairs because B & Q told us we could and let us have the gear, no questions, just as if we were real builders and decorators.

Bryan shows us how. Not content with the ironic deco look of 1975, Bryan takes us on a decade and reveals exactly what early eighties good taste means.

What a change from the stuffed, accretion-filled hardware shops of our past, staffed by professional fifty-year-old sceptics in dun-coloured work coats! What a change after the horrors of the builders' merchants ('You can have it, but you gotta buy at least three hundredweight')! It all fitted in with that heady feeling of change, experiment, no limits.

There was magazine madness, too, propelling the whole thing forward, taking care of the theoretical, as opposed to the practical, side. Obviously your *House & Garden* and your *Homes & Gardens* were around, as they always had been. But in a flurry of activity, we suddenly got *Designer's Data* (first published, 1985); *Design Week* (1986); *Blueprint* (1983); *Country Homes & Interiors* (1986); and the one, the only, the greatest, *The World Of Interiors*, which first saw the light of day in 1981. It's hard to overestimate the impact that *Interiors* had when it first appeared: glamourously produced,

richly materialistic and narrow-minded to the point of hedonism, it was the kind of magazine you could imagine Joris Huysmans subscribing to, if only he'd lived.

As with B & Q and its hard-core DIY ethos, the service *Interiors* and its fellow publications provided was partly information, partly flattery. They didn't tell us that we *ought* to take an interest (an obsessive, semi-demented interest) in style, form, the look – they told us that *we'd been interested all along* and that only now had the magazine biz caught up with *us*. Creative geniuses, we were: at last, everyone could hold an opinion about magnolia.

Living Over The Bank

It didn't stop there, though. Not only were we interior designers, we were also, necessarily, men and women of business – specifically, *we were all property speculators* – we had capital. If we owned a place, we spent a good deal of time thinking of it purely as an asset and wondering how fast it was appreciating and was it ahead of the market and had we seen an investment opportunity, or had we bought in too late… which was great, in its way. It added a nice, crunchy real-world sort of texture to something which would otherwise have been a little too easy, a little too much frippery and fun, if there hadn't been some sort of hard financial issue underpinning it; it made it altogether more manly.

But if you're talking assets, you're talking liquidity, and if you're talking liquidity, you're talking markets. A schism here: we weren't the market-makers, and we weren't going to be the market-makers no matter how much we prided ourselves on our property speculator acumen (don't forget that in a high-inflation market, everyone looks clever). The market makers were the *real* real estate boys and girls, the *property consultants*. And weren't *they* having fun?

(Listen, where did this *property consultant* thing come from, anyway? Once upon a time, estate agents were just house-sellers – either your high-tone, advert-in-the-front-pages-of-*Country Life*, offers-invited-for-the-freehold merchants with old, good suits and a hint of not having been quite bright enough to stick it in the Guards; or small-time suburbanites with dreams of having the biggest Riley in the golf club car park, while they tried to shift pattern-book stuff out in distant suburbs somewhere.)

The young property people had learnt a lot from the City boys and girls. They knew that a market wasn't fenced in by the gritty reality of the things being bought and sold, by the solid linkage of supply and demand: rather, it had to have a *mood*, an urgent, overwhelming collective desire to head towards the same goal. It could have been tulip-mania in seventeenth-century Holland; it could have been the South Sea Bubble in eighteenth-century England; it *was* the London Stock Market all the way through to 1987; and it was the UK house market in the eighties, start to finish. Between 1985 and 1989, average house prices in the UK more than *doubled.* Everybody had to have a piece of the action, and the market-makers and facilitators – those intermediaries we used to call estate agents – were there to keep the turnover brisk and the appetites keen ('Hell's bells, it was fun. I don't regret it.'). Rather as with the interior designers, it suddenly turned out that everyone seemed to know someone who was involved in property.

There was something else the property boys and girls picked up from the City, too: the fine art of selling out. Just as the directors of the little broking and jobbing outfits in the Square Mile found themselves being bought up by American, Swiss and British big-time institutions around the time of Big Bang, so your well-placed, well-established estate agents found themselves being courted by all sorts of unlikely people who wanted to establish a presence in the property market. Chain estate agencies, sporting uniform exteriors and designed house styles, started to emerge from the heterogeneous mish-mash that had gone before. By 1986, the craze for buy-outs and buy-ins was reaching something of a peak, with Hambro Countryside temporarily the biggest player in the new world of estate agents' *chains*, sitting (as they were) on 350 offices around the UK. Lloyd's Black Horse Agencies were up to 219, while Prudential Property were third, with 113 nationwide offices.

Naturally, these huge money combines weren't terribly interested in the take from buying and selling properties, however aerated the market might have been at the time. No, what they wanted were tied outlets for their finance *products* – all the mortgages, insurance policies, endowment schemes and what-have-you that provided a *real* income and which the hapless home speculator would only end up accepting off some spiv independent financial adviser if the big boys didn't get to him or her first. Given that just about everyone in the land seemed to want to shackle themselves to the real estate roundabout of investment and profiteering (Britain was earning for itself at this time the reputation of Country With More Home Ownership Than Anywhere Else In Europe), it made sense for the bosses of the Pru and Lloyds Bank and so on to buy into this business – even if it meant paying out millions to a very slightly undeserving knot of middle-aged freehold floggers who must have thought it was Christmas all of a sudden. The real costs, the hidden pay-offs, were not to emerge until some time later. But in 1986, the world just looked like that.

So you had your house, your interior design, your property adviser keeping you abreast of the lastest undervalued equities in the housing market, your little piece of the action in one of Britain's burgeoning villages, but wasn't something missing from the story? Wasn't there some unexplored aspect of being heavily into property and design and lifestyle? What *was* it, exactly?

The Final Frontier; A Greener Dream

The *countryside*: that was what was missing. Of course! If the city was being carved up into fictitious villages-within-villages, why not turn the whole thing on its head and get a stake in a *real* village? Why *not*? What could the let's-do-it *zeitgeist* not acheive? Having opened up the most distant reaches of the Victorian suburbs, caused a new city to arise in the wastes of Docklands, reclaimed the council house, re-invented high-rise living and shown that everywhere is redeemable and nothing is impossible… why not take a look at the outlying districts and see what can be done with them? Why not explore Greater London, Greater Manchester? Bucks, Oxon, Glos, Wilts, *Norfolk*… they're all out there and they're *full of properties*….

London had, of course, been expanding into the Home Counties and East Anglia and the south coast and the Cotswolds for decades. For heaven's sake, the old Metropolitan Line (of Metroland) goes as far as Amersham, Bucks, and had done since before the war. Brighton had been London-by-the-sea since the last century. England south of Newmarket and west of Gloucester is really all London – London-centred, London-peopled, London-thinking – and has been so for a long time. But in the eighties it took on a new closeness, a new accessibility, once people made that little mental *volte-face* that allowed them to think of the world in time rather than distance.

Time was a big thing, by 1983, anyway. It was becoming clear that time was in increasingly short supply, what with the pressure of work, the money that had to be made and the splendid new things you could spend your money on in the periods when you weren't actually earning it. From 1985 onwards, we began to get more and more obsessed with the toys of the age – mobile 'phones, in-car faxes, Sony Walkmen and tiny TVs, lap-top computers – because they said that we were well-heeled *busy* people, people whose time was in short supply: we needed these things, these conveniences, these time-savers, to live our hectic lives. But as well as allowing us to fill our precious time, they made it possible to manage our time. We started to think much more creatively about the parcels of time which made up the day – and once we'd started to think of, say, a two-hour commute as an opportunity (to listen to music on that dinky new Walkman, do some reading, check up on one's holiday arrangements, shred some paperwork) rather than a penance, so it became clear that we could live somewhere wholly new and different, because the extra time involved in living somewhere new and different wasn't going to go to waste.

So then the question was: where? Obviously, you didn't want to spend more time churning to and from home than you needed to, but you wanted somewhere nice, all the same. So, at one extremity of the London orbit, you had your Cotswolds: an hour and 20 minutes by train into Paddington, an hour and a half (God willing, and let's hope it's not fouled up around Heathrow) down the M4. Stroud, Kemble, Swindon stations: all started to service the masses of hungry new village-seekers who wanted to go out and get some rural quality while they still could.

Kemble, a sweet little golden-stoned railway station (like a tiny Oxford college from some angles) just outside Cirencester, suddenly found itself deluged with busy, busy passengers, catching the 6.30 run in the morning and back again at 10.00 at night. Providing a direct service into town, and surrounded by some of the prettiest bits of Gloucestershire, Kemble went in the space of a few years from being nowhere special, to the Waterloo of the Cotswolds. Unlike Waterloo, however, it also offered the mixed

attractions of Prince Charles, Princess Anne and Jilly Cooper. In fact, if you played your cards right, it even offered you the chance to be in one of Jilly's books.

Issue One of *Country Living*: the rural life brought to your town doorstep. Dried flowers in baskets.

Jilly Cooper's alternative: countryside for Londoners.

In the other direction, you had Cambridge, Stowmarket and Diss, providing East Anglian country relief for the questing Londoner. As the process matured, and the nearer, nicer properties got snatched up, even Lincolnshire and Yorkshire started to be colonized. Hebden Bridge – *Hebden Bridge*, for God's sake – got itself a name as one of London's most extreme commuter destinations: it was pleasant, it was within reach of Doncaster or Leeds railway stations, it was a mere 200 miles from London, and the price of a two-bed cottage in Hebden went up 60 per cent in two years.

This was, again, something new. This was an extreme discipline at work – far more than the conventional annexation of Kent and Surrey, which the City's bankers and brokers had been making use of for years. This was an exploration of new territories (… everywhere is redeemable…), coupled with the property speculator's hunger for a bargain to be clawed out. After all, if you could sell your three-bed terraced job in London SW6 and spend the proceeds on a *manor house* (with five acres, a paddock and some very seriously mullioned drawing-room windows), why not do it? Just to make it easier, there was a blitz of new-wave country lifestyle magazines to let all the townies know how straightforward it was when you got there: *County* (1988); *Country Walking* (1987); *Country Living* (1985); *Country Homes & Interiors* (1986) – all peddling a dream which may or may not have had anything to do with 'real' country life (*Country Life*, of course, being for the over-forties serious money only) but which looked as cute as a button, viewed from the grimy fastness of the metropolis.

At the same time, the value discrepancies between London housing and everywhere else, plus the ease with which you could borrow money against the inflated worth of your London home, meant that startlingly large numbers of people – 220 000 by the end of the decade, according to one estimate – could buy second homes. These were usually quaint rustic hovels or gamekeepers' one-up one-downers, which were then extended and thatched and plumbed into submission to bring them up to weekend getaway class. What was a hen house in 1981 could be done up to within an inch of its life and flogged in 1988 for £145 000. Depending on where you stood, this was either good news for the rural community – bringing work for the local artisans and reclaiming properties which would otherwise have returned to the earth; or bad news – driving up the prices of small, affordable homes and keeping the local artisans and farm workers out of the properties which were rightly theirs.

But it was also very slightly mad, this hunt for the second home, the wellington-ed foot in the country. And in that respect, it started to say something worrying about the property party as a whole... .

Just think of the time equation again: with hindsight, a lot of people now see that while you could manage your time and energy efficiently enough to make it worth plugging down the M4 or the A20 on a Friday night and back again on a Sunday, just to be among the hedgerows... it wasn't entirely rational. As Nicholas Coleridge recently observed: 'It is not unusual to spend a total of eight hours on the road simply getting to and from a weekend cottage... ' That's a whole working day, jammed up, breathing exhausts, squabbling with the girlfriend/kids/wife's friend you didn't want to ask, sitting virtually immobile in your car. A *whole day*. At first, it didn't stop anyone, mind you. But it did suggest one way in which things were getting just a wee bit out of hand, a wee bit *overdone* in the craze to *own*... .

On The Boil

As did the Broom Cupboard. Now we *all* remember the Broom Cupboard – that one-roomed flat up for sale in London's Brompton Road, in early 1987, with the follwing

dimensions: 5 ft wide by 11 ft long, plus a lavatory/shower, 2 ft square. It was in a mansion block and, yes, it had been a broom cupboard, before conversion. The asking price was £36 500. *That* broom cupboard. Ideal for the person (or persons – why not? Maybe two co-habiting contortonists with a taste for the good things of life.) who basically needs a bedroom in town, somewhere to crash out before going out and about (the Pivotelli wall-mounted TV support was really what

Knightsbridge capsule living for less than £40 000 – the ex-broom cupboard.

this little notion was all about; it couldn't have happened without it). It worked OK for students in the old hall of residence. Why not do it again?

Well, there's nothing specifically wrong with living in a space 5 x 11 ft, especially if you've got Harrods and the V & A and Hyde Park and the Oratory and so on around to keep you company. There's nothing inherently bad about living in a coffin-shaped slot or overnighting in a Tokyo capsule hotel or calling a shoebox your own: but at £36 500, that kind of inconvenience comes a trifle dear, wouldn't you say?

Yes, it was expensive, but not uniquely so. In October 1988, a single room, 9ft 4in x 9ft 2in, went for sale in Tufnell Park at £55 000. In 1987, a studio flat in Holland Park went on the market at £160 000 ('With a little work,' said the proud freeholder, 'it could be very chic.'). The same year, an unfinished six-bed apartment in Bermondsey went out for £2 million. In mid 1988, Regalian – the property developers who gave us Battersea Village and the Falcons, a couple of knackered inner-London council estates made over and flogged to the new rich – put Florin Court, in the middle of the City, up for grabs after spending £2 million smartening the place up. There were eighty-four refurbished flats for sale (plus a pool, sauna and parking) and they went within two hours of the sales office opening. Eight million quid's worth of sales, two hours' work, *done. Loved* the *hype.*

But was anyone actually going to live there? To be honest, that was hardly the question to ask, in those frantic last months of property madness. It was quite clearly the thing to buy first and use later. Rent it out and sell it on. Or not even rent it – just hang on for a year or so and offload it on the ever-upward market. Properties turned into gaming chips – and in an inflating market like this one, inflation would get you out of any errors of judgement you happened to make. Sad, in a way, that the need to live somewhere *new* – to *explore* that dream of the early eighties – should have wound up like this, but that's the way things go in a mature market. Not that anyone was doing anything quite so wildly speculative down in the London villages, mind you. It wasn't quite the same in Battersea and Stoke Newington – not quite so liquid, you might say. But elsewhere, things were selling off-plan, the property hustlers were moving shells and condo concepts, while the buyers were thinking of themselves as yet another layer of intermediary, with, somewhere along the line, an end-user who might actually go and live in the square footage that was at the heart of it all.

It was all happening around the first half of 1988: looking back on it, that was when the heat was at its highest. House prices in the UK rose by 30 per cent in the first six months of that year.

As it turned out, it was really the rapture of the deep: something dreadful was happening beneath the euphoria. And you know how it is with money....

... And Over The Top

Back in what passes for the real world Chancellor Nigel Lawson brought out his spring budget for 1988, in the conventional fashion – and simultaneously started to unravel all the dreams of the crazy speculators, the mortgage freaks, the market facilitators, the home designers and the home-owners who'd jacked themselves up to the nth degree with borrowings against their properties. *What did he do?* Basically, he halved mortgage interest relief (aka MIRAS) for unmarried couples; and removed mortgage interest completely on home improvement loans. In other words, your breezily unwed co-owners (two men, as it might be) who were *each* collecting interest relief on the first £30 000 of their mortgage, found that this little bonus had been cut in two. And all those of us who were taking out £20 000 loans from the banks and the building societies and the mortgage brokers in order to turn the loft into a spare bedroom (but in reality taking a little time out in the Seychelles on the proceeds) found that there was no tax break on that little scam any more.

Then again, how much difference would this really have made, do you think? A few unmarried couples maybe decide not to go in together on that pad in Chelsea? The kitchen extension stays unmodernized for another eighteen months? I mean, how many people are we really talking about here? Well, the size of the target audience was revealed when the good Chancellor explained – on the advice of the Inland Revenue, as he was subsequently keen to point out – that despite everything, multiple mortgage interest relief would stay in place for four months after the budget, on account of the Revenue being unable to get their computers working in time. In other words, everyone had until 1 August to get their feet in the door of some place, somewhere, *anywhere*, in order to qualify for the Last Of The Great Tax Breaks.

And so they went crazy. Now *why* do you think property prices rose at an average rate of 30 per cent in the first six months of 1988? Because there were so many people screaming to get in there before multiple mortgage interest relief ended. Did it matter that by doing so, they pushed up house prices so far that they could never claw back in tax breaks what they were having to lay out on the properties in the first place? *Do* these things matter in a property frenzy? Of course not. Only....

Well, first you had the end of MIRAS for unmarried couples. And then you had interest rates up to 13 per cent at the end of 1988 and still rising, on account of a nasty outbreak of inflation. Double digit base rates: a gun at the market's head. Remember that at around this time, house prices were, on average, stuck at a ratio of five times earnings, with plenty of good people servicing mortgages of £100 000 or £150 000. (In London's Docklands, by the way, there was already a certain amount of unease as a result of the stockmarket crash of 1987: in some cases, as many as 10 per cent of purchasers who had exchanged contracts on off-plan-style Docklands properties, defaulted in the 12 months following the crash. Developers found themselves having to drop prices by as much as £10 000 a unit, to keep the market moving.)

It took a while, mark you, for the dream to unravel completely. As J. K. Galbraith puts it, 'The momentum built up by a good boom is not dissipated in a moment.' In 1988 and 1989, there was still plenty of noise being made about whacky property purchases (converted Presbyterian churches; a house only 7 ft 9 in wide, on sale at £115 000) and still enough interest in luscious newly-built service appartments to keep things moving along. But the world was definitely going to go *down* rather than *up*. And anyone who got into the market just at the end of the boom, was discovering how beastly it could all be out there.

The more speculative the property, of course, the harder things were: in Docklands, it was not unheard-of for a new purpose-built appartment to lose 25-30 per cent of its value in the time between the initial contracts being signed, and completion, a couple of years later. Your £120 000 dream deal of 1987 finally got a front door and a bit of carpeting some time in 1989, by which time it was worth £85 000. Speculative and more speculative – the Knightsbridge Cupboard going for £36 500, later sold for £15 000... Out in Hoxton and the wildernesses of Dorset and Lincolnshire, those essential country cottages and lifestyle barns began to stick and then drift down, as their owners retrenched in the face of double-digit mortgage rates... *negative equity*: the language of the deal, the double-speak of the would-be amateur property speculator, came back in a sinister, transformed guise... and those die-hards who'd been talking area, area, area, while everyone else bought dreams, started to look unpleasantly complacent....

So after all the *voltes-faces* of the eighties, are we back with yet another *volte-face* (well, who'd have guessed it?), back into the world of grey properties in safe, grey areas, properties bought and paid for by their end-users, with all the possibilities of the great eighties Property Party lost and forgotten?

Staying On

Not exactly. For a start, Docklands is still there, bloodied but just about standing. The insane little Docklands Light Railway (a driverless electric railway which made the automatic shuttle service between North and South Terminals of Gatwick Airport look sophisticated) has slowly and painfully put on weight, and now resembles a public transport system more closely than it used to – which is a good sign for the area as a whole. If you can at least get in and out, it does become a little more real, a little less *conceptual*. Butler's Wharf, on the south side of the Thames, is up and running. Cascades is still there, as is Chelsea Harbour. These things won't evaporate, necessarily; nor will the middle-class *arrivistes* of Stockwell, Kennington, West Ham and the Goldhawk Road, although they may find themselves, in these impoverished times, having to be rather more resourceful about the necessities of life than they originally intended.

Interiors is still going, too, and Kemble Station still has a good clientele, who never moved back. And no one at present has any plans to remove council tenants' right to buy, no matter how many cheeky renters there are, pointing their fingers at the freeholders and laughing. These things are still in the air, still something to think about… and yes, everywhere is *still* redeemable; but it might take a little longer than we thought.

The fall-out is in the confidence – but then that's what happens when a boom market goes down. It'll come up again – but probably never so far – because the commodity at the heart of it all, the *thing desired* is still desirable. But between now and then, we have to go through the nightmare of repossessions and negative equity – penalties which are more painful than losses on the Stock Market, because they affect us so directly: as one eighties property buyer said, 'We knew in our *minds* that whatever property we bought, was going to grow in value and our wealth was going to increase. The reality of course is somewhat different….'

P L U T O C R A T S

There was a time – we're going back a long way, here – when the City of London was just a bit *boring*. In 1963, *Queen* magazine (as it then was) ran a piece called 'Are You Still Something If You're Something In The City?' Evidently not, when at the time you could also have been one of the Beatles or Sean Connery or David Bailey. 'There is no sex within the City limits,' sneered *Queen*. City types were taxidermied old parties in bowler hats. *Punch* cartoons used them as a permanent shorthand for everything that was against the *zeitgeist*: Conservative, unglamorous, old. Why be in the City when you could be out, being young and cool?

London EC4, The Cool Zone

But: 25 years later, and what'd happened? The City of London, the Square Mile, was now so hip, so central to the collective imagination, that not only had hundreds of thousands of words been ladled on it in the tabloids and the broadsheets and the

The old brigade – pavement talk for clubbable types with traditional kit.

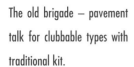

Boesky goes Hollywood: Gekko dealing in dynamic braces.

colour magazines (*Tatler* and *Harpers & Queen*, as it now was, both being conspicuous for buying massively into the subject), but good person and popular Left-winger Caryl Churchill opened a huge, hit musical called *Serious Money* (music and lyrics: Ian Dury plus some key Blockheads), with OK young playwright Tony Marchant launching his well-reviewed play, *Speculators*, on the subject a few months later.

On top of which, Paramount had a film hit with their Wall Street-derived comedy, *Trading Places*, after which American Entertainment had an even bigger film hit with the Michael Douglas vehicle *Wall Street*, which in turn inspired the British Euston Films to produce the City of London-centred *Dealers*, which, despite being a turkey, was considered such a hot notion that Euston kept the hugely expensive trading-floor set from the film to build a TV drama series around it, *Capital City*.

The City had taken hold of our minds: City buildings (now thrusting, futuristic) lurked in the backgrounds of car promotions, insurance commercials, *moderne* electric cooker ads – symbolizing wealth, power, *tomorrow*. City practices – up-all-hours work sessions, spontaneous deal-making, eating and drinking and wassailing in the smartest environments – set a benchmark by which the rest of us decided what kind of lives we were living. The Financial Square Mile had become a magnet for people's dreams and demonologies. It even set clothing fashions. And anyone young and even half-bright worked out that the City was a repository of pure cash for those who wanted it badly enough and that, like sex, you're best at it when you're the right side of thirty. So how did we get *there*?

Unlike so many eighties changes, the City's hectic launch into the public's imagination, was not a direct result of government policy. In fact, the City and the Tory Party were ever so slightly leery of each other, despite the fact that the City itself is constitutionally and monstrously Conservative in its politics. The City was something of a law unto itself and only really got into the big frame when something insane happened, like the South Sea Bubble of 1720, the Clarence Hatry fraud of 1929, or the crash of the Johnson Matthey Bank in 1984. The rest of the time, frankly, it was just there, distinctly shy of the spotlight, adding to Britain's invisible exports and financing various largeish businesses through loans and stocks and shares.

New Jobs For New Boys... And Girls

By the beginning of the decade, though, something was definitely in the air. Big Bang and all that were still a long way off, but already, university graduates were noticing that while the rest of British industry and commerce was shrinking at a horrible rate and that the jobs had gone with them, the City was recruiting quite handsomely. Your Cambridge maths undergraduate would turn up for the university milk round, get a job offer to do something normal, like work at ICL (remember ICL? Big British computer makers? Then the British Leyland of computing, now Japanese-owned.), find that in the six months between getting the job offer and graduating, ICL had decided to axe their entire graduate intake for the year, and in a mood of well-screw-this, would pitch up at a City institution of some kind (maybe one of the new, American ones) and – get a job right away. This was 1981, maybe, and he'd start off on something fairly basic, like £4500 a year.

But something was in the air… the Bank of England had registered that unless London did something to deregulate and globalize and become competitive, it would lose its key role as one of the world's top three financial trading centres, so handily dead-centre between Tokyo and New York. So the Bank actually lobbied the government on behalf of the City: and Lord Cockfield (Treasury Minister) and Cecil Parkinson (then Secretary of State for Trade and Industry) actually listened. And then the Office of Fair Trading threatened to bring an action in 1983, forcing the Stock Exchange to abandon its practice of setting fixed commissions (yes! the Arctic breeze of competition entered the City's soul!) which meant that all of a sudden, a lot of little broking firms were going to have to reorganize into some much bigger ones; while at the same time, outside share-holders (i.e. very Big Banks) were being allowed to take larger and larger stakes in the City firms; exchange controls had already been abolished in 1979, allowing shares to be traded internationally; and from the early eighties onwards, anyone could trade on the Stock Exchange and the Gilts market… which meant that from out of the blue, these seething American, Swiss and Hong Kong-based do-it-all financial monsters could just *land* in the middle of London and go to work, running books on more or less anything that moved. Go global. *And this wasn't even Big Bang.*

The upshot was that between 1981 and 1984, London managed to lose 90 000 jobs in the manufacturing sector, but generate 45 000 jobs in the financial one. And a lot of these jobs were all about *trading* – buying and flogging company shares and bonds – some gilts too, but those were pretty boring – and seeing what sort of turn you could make on the deal. The amount of purely speculative trading (doing it on your own account – on the firm's account – as opposed to doing it for an outside client) went through the roof. The big players had *lots* of money to trade with – that was the point of being big. The market was *liquid*. The Stock Exchange Index (initially, the old FT Top 30; subsequently, the FTSE, or Financial Times 100 Share Index) zapped through 600 for the first time in its life in 1982. In August of that year, the Great Wall Street Bull Market started: one investment fund, run by US brokers Merrill Lynch, would grow by 486 per cent in five years. *Get in there* – in time for Big Bang!

Big Bang

Which was what, exactly? Well, it was the day in October 1986, when the old Stock Exchange went into mothballs and all the dealers and traders and market-makers who'd been on the floor, the picture they always showed, disappeared into these hangar-sized dealing rooms, built into the offices of the new City integrated investment houses.

Up until October 1986, if you wanted to trade in stocks and shares, your broker had to go physically onto the floor of the Stock Exchange (rather a fascinating space, the size of several football pitches and kitted out in beige) which had been built for

Ten years at four and a half over base – *and he bought it!* New brigade: limo talk.

this purpose in 1970, and walk up to a jobber. Now, a jobber was basically a used car dealer who had shares instead of old Talbot Horizons and Ford Escorts. Brokers would come along and try to sell shares to a jobber, who'd take them at whatever price he thought was right. Then he'd sit on them until another broker turned up, wanting to buy. So he'd sell them at a profit. To do this, all the jobbers had to stand at pitches, like racecourse bookies, these doubtful beings in suits, lounging around their beige plastic pitches (a bit like those drum-shaped advertising pillars you find in the streets of Paris) and the whole thing in essence, hadn't changed since the eighteenth century.

That was on the way out, *seriously* on the way out. After Big Bang, it was all going to be done on a computer system called SEAQ (Stock Exchange Automated Quotations) and the jobbers and the brokers were all going to be part of the same firms (a conflict of interest, here? *Absolutely not.* This was the City, boy: My Word Is My Bond, all that stuff, remember?) which had amalgamated by now into these bizarre-sounding collectives, with names like Citicorp Scrimgeour Vickers and Barclays de Zoete Wedd, clanking, bolted-together names, names that sounded like Dutch army commands. What's more, these collectives were spending around £5000 per square foot on equipping the dealing rooms with all the latest toys – screens, software, miles of underfloor cabling that made sixties City buildings unlettable overnight – so you could see, hear, smell that this was an astronomically large endeavour... Sucking in the boys and girls at a tremendous rate.

Hip, Young Gunslingers Wanted

The City wanted you young and it wanted you *now*. It wanted you young because that meant you'd be more likely to have a degree (from Warwick University – strong maths faculty; from Sheffield – good on Japanese) for the analytical stuff; or young because you were straight out of Hackney Downs Comprehensive and you were sharp as a tack and didn't want to go to college *and* you had the energy to work like a maniac, ten hours a day at the dealers' screens, for the next eight years. As the Bang grew closer, the need for young bodies grew even more urgent. Your disillusioned ICL reject joined up in 1981, on £4500 a year with the prospects of something better in a few years' time. But a couple of years later, Warburgs said they were offering trainee investment bankers £13 500 plus banking benefits, straight off. Some banks were offering their new recruits a straight £2000 cash bonus *just for joining*. Then, spend a couple of years with a decent firm as an equities analyst, you were looking at, what? £75 000 a year, plus a German car, plus BUPA?

Everywhere you turned, there were signs that the City wanted you, needed you, and was going out of its way to make itself attractive to you. A hundred million pounds of computer equipment was levered into the City in a couple of years, just for the boys and girls to play on. The wine bars sprouted and expanded and glossed themselves up at an exponential rate. And at the height of the madness, between 1985 and 1987, some 60 000 financial jobs were created, out of the ether.

INTERVIEW

LORD YOUNG

Former Secretary of State for the Department of Trade and Industry

Q Lord Young what exactly is enterprise?

A Enterprise is the desire of people to go and work for themselves, to set up their new businesses, and it is the foundation of modern economies.

Q Why did we need it in the eighties?

A We had gone through twenty or thirty years – the fifties, the sixties and the seventies – in which the tax system and the climate had stopped new businesses starting, and when we went though unemployment in the early eighties we knew that all companies, because of technology, would shed labour, and we had to get new businesses started. So, from back in the days of the Manpower Services Commission... we were really trying to get new businesses started and we got hundreds of thousands of new businesses. Then we had to encourage them to grow.

Q. How did you do that fostering?

A We started programmes called the Enterprise Allowance Scheme [where] unemployed people were encouraged to commute their benefit for a year and get some money and start working for themselves... Then when I came over to DTI in 1987, I knew... we had to take that forward so I looked round to find other sorts of programmes to encourage these small businesses to grow to become medium ones.

Q Who was your target – what people were you aiming at?

A Specifically, in the DTI, to a quarter of a million people. People who were directors of small medium-size firms that we needed to make larger firms... Every company in the world, started off as a one-man business and it grew, and... one in a thousand grow to be medium-sized [and] one in ten thousand grow to be a giant. But they grow and then they die because businesses are organic. You have to have [the] birth of new businesses, and we lacked them starting in the past so we had to accelerate in a rush.

Q You started this policy of fostering enterprise, how did it work?

A Well, first of all, you had to give people self confidence... You see in the United States the role models are the successful people, they're the people that everyone looks up to. In this country at that time, and perhaps it hasn't changed very much, we tended to look up to the pop star, the soccer player, people who made money that way rather than those who made money through setting up their own businesses. We do have people like Alan Sugar, we have people like Richard Branson and others... But I wanted us to have lots more and to get the idea across. So when we started the Enterprise Initiative – which was there to encourage small medium-size firms to become more professional, more able in marketing in quality – we based it on stories of successful companies, companies that started off small, like Phileas Fogg, that grew, that went up.

Q Now one of your responsibilities was the City, and the huge change that took place in the City. What was it for?

A The City has now become the leading financial centre in Europe. You look at the German and the Dutch banks that have now come into the city of London. Frankfurt won't take over from London. London evolved and changed in time... Forget whether there's a single currency and all the other things – the City of London is now going to be the financial heart of Europe and that's very important for us. If we hadn't gone through that process, hadn't made the city more entrepreneurial, less old boy more open to all talents, that wouldn't have happened.

Q Privatization?

A Yes. I'm very proud of privatization... Take the industry I'm in today, telecommunications. You know a dozen years ago BT gave you a choice of two telephones, something called a trim-phone or nothing. They came when they were ready. Today, if you want a telephone and ring up they come running, the service is good... Why? Because of competition. And privatization is not really about ownership, whether the state owns it or not, it's about accountability, it's about whether the chairman can be sacked. In the old nationalized industry· if you made a mistake you were probably put in the House of Lords. Today, if you don't do it properly, you go... You see we started – unfortunately we started nationalization as well – but we certainly started privatization, and now the companies that were privatized early on have grown out of all recognition.

Q Well, lots of people say that privatization was a way of shifting funds around in fancy ways and enriching the City and enriching the government coffers but not enriching anybody else, and using assets that had formerly been public assets – and acquired with public money and so on. How did you feel about those criticisms?

A Yes, they would say that wouldn't they, but nobody in their right mind can compare the service that they actually get today out of the once-privatized industries with the services they had fifteen years ago. And if you think it's got nothing to do with privatization you go to France and you go to Germany, and you see how quickly they respond to customers. Today, the customer is king.

Q Is there one image, one person, one event, that sums up that spirit of the late eighties for you?

A I'm not sure I can think of one person. It was a general feeling that we were, we could make it... If you went overseas, the way people regarded the United Kingdom then in the late eighties was a way they hadn't regarded it since the War. We were a nation on the way up, we were a nation that was gaining. The Japanese came here because they knew we had the best get up and go. And today we've transformed this country.

Gorgeous Gotham City

Just to add to the excitement, were these incredible, wholly un-English *buildings*, coming out of the ground, replacing the Forsytes' discreet Edwardian stone ramparts. There was Standard Chartered's colossal glass-fronted thing in Old Broad Street, a microwave the size of an airship hanger, filled with huge trees from the forests of Borneo. There was Number 1, Finsbury Avenue, Warburgs' new home, a great, brooding black and brown metal lattice. There was the huge, glamorous new Broadgate development just behind that, with its positively decadent use of marble and its skating-rink in the centre. And there was Richard Rogers' completely amazing new Lloyd's Building, opened in 1986 and costing, well, in the region of £200 million. There were so many *atria* springing up in the crystal palaces of London EC, all infested with rainforests and modern sculpture, it was like being in a Max Ernst painting. Combine this with the NatWest Tower, the Bank of England, the Royal Exchange and the Leadenhall Market and you have… the perfect imagined city, weird, diverse – yet driven by one thing… the unembarrassed, the *shameless* desire for money… So we all stared, hypnotized by the radioactive glow of cash: a Stock Market worth £250 billion by the end of 1985… £180 billion of bank lending… gilts worth £127 billion… all on our doorstep, all in this hot little Square Mile….

So it looked amazing, and it was clearly worth an absolute fortune. But the City was hypnotically interesting not just for the surface gloss (although that *was* hypnotically interesting, in its own right). Just an inch or so below the surface, some terribly British issues were being fought out.

Toffs and Yobs

Like toffs and yobs, for instance. One of the things that was so satisfying about the City, for all the features writers and colour prose specialists who descended on it from the dailies, was that it contained a complete, ossified class structure, dating back to the previous century. It was like opening a locked door in the V & A and discovering a forgotten collection of artifacts from the Napoleonic Wars, or Victoria's Diamond Jubilee.

It turned out, to everyone's amazement, that there were places like Cazenoves, the inexpressably smart stockbroking

So big, so thought-through, so un-English… At the Broadgate development you could go ice-skating, eat gravadlax, admire your reflection in the mirror-smooth marble floor and spend the morning in your office making a killing on BT shares. Work as play; money as happiness.

INTERVIEW

PETER DE SAVARY

Entrepreneur

Q So have things changed that much since the eighties?

A Yes, I think things have changed quite a lot. I think people are much more conservative. I think there're more cautious. People are looking for better value for money and generally in business the margins are smaller.

Q It sounds duller, doesn't it?

A I don't know that it's duller. It's keener on your wits and it's more of a challenge really. People are less casual than they were in the eighties.

Q You clearly had a very, very exciting life in the eighties reading the clips? Quite amazing. Think back before the eighties. What was life like then? What was your life like before the eighties?

A In the seventies of course, we were in a recession as well. I mean the recession of 1974 lasted for several years – in fact, right up till the eighties. It was pretty flat… I was heavily engaged in the oil industry and the oil business, as you know, in the seventies was a growing and booming business… I was in the right business at the right time.

Q But you weren't famous then were you? We sort of heard about you in the eighties?

A I think probably the America's Cup as much as anything in the early eighties is what gave me a little bit of a profile. That was something that, until my involvement in it, had been a fairly low key event in terms of UK media coverage and what we tried to do was make it a great British adventure.

Q It wasn't just that. You were being famous all the time?

A Some attention was drawn to the fact that, that I did buy Land's End and John O'Groats. And people were intrigued by that.

Q If somebody asked you in 1980 what it was you did what would you have said?

A What I say today and what I've always said: I'm an entrepreneur. I'm a somebody who takes risks, usually a calculated risk and I try to do something that perhaps other people haven't thought of doing and sometimes it works and, indeed, sometimes it doesn't work.

Q Was the eighties the right time for people like you?

A Yes, I think the eighties was a period where things would go up in value almost automatically over relatively short periods of time. It was a period where access to capital and debt-financing was very easy.

Q How are you different as a businessman from the eighties? Has it changed you at all?

A I think the fact of being a few years older, now in my fifties and having suffered a number of embarrassments and losses during the eighties and that all being fairly publicly aired and discussed, obviously tempers you on the side of conservatism and caution.

firm (smart for a stockbroker's, that is; the meanest merchant bank was of course generically smarter than any stockbroker) where partners of the firm were still allowed to give their sons a job in the outfit, *as of right*. It was called 'bringing someone to the front door'. The senior partner at Cazenoves in the mid-eighties merited a place in *Burke's Peerage*. Cazenoves told their clients that they would be *allowed* a certain number of shares in a company, when the time came to deliver. While the rest of Britain was experiencing things like the Depression and World War Two and the Welfare State and Socialism and what have you, Cazenoves were living in another time dimension. What happened to that missing century...?

At the same time, there was this weird, post-feudal quality to the work in the square mile. There were grandees, aspirant grandees, a tiny middle class (usually with some sort of dreary professional skill involving computers or accountancy) and then a rabble of serfs, drawn from all over the East End, to feed Moloch at the battery-pen trading stations or on the floor of the London International Financial Futures Exchange (the setting for *Serious Money*). It was as if all modern, progressive social change, the business of the Labour party since 1893, had been *frozen*. The class divisions were completely staggering. Them and Us were written in letters a mile high, down every street, in every doorway. Posh chaps got panelled boardrooms and beautiful wool suits and proper signet rings and patronized crushingly old-fashioned restaurants that dished up boiling coronary food; yobs (separated by no more than a wall, but at the same time, a thousand miles away) got sweaty chipboard work stations, grimy white socks, horrible shat-upon pubs and winebars where they got arsed out their heads... And red Ferraris.

And this was the other old issue: was money really a dirty word for us demoralized British? Because here, it wasn't the kind of money the rest of us knew about, the kind that there was never quite enough of, the kind that you desperately wanted to know about but could never bring yourself to mention, the kind of money that was, in itself, a vaguely prurient subject, like hives. Here, in the City, money was like water – the essence of being. You handled it, you lived it, you talked about it *all the time* and at the end of everything, when the battery-pen finally let you quit at night, you went out and made damn sure that you enjoyed some of the things that only money could provide. Like Dom Perignon, three weeks in Phuket and those flame-red Ferraris.

It was *liberating*: the rest of the world peered into this rockpool and found that, on the one hand, Society As We Know It hadn't changed much since 1381; but on the other hand, it didn't seem to matter, *because money made it all right*. It seemed to have transfiguring properties. It allowed this terrible state of affairs to continue and flourish, so that everyone was happy, because everyone at heart loved the same thing. And – even weirder – it transfigured the people who *had* the money. Not so much the grandees and public school slugs, who gave the impression (however much they denied it in print) of spending just twenty minutes too long over their oysters and Chablis, of leaving just an hour too early on Friday evenings, and of being just a bit too nauseatingly full of themselves the rest of the time. No, it transfigured the sweating East End wideboys, the dealers and traders.

They were still, quite clearly, pinheaded yobs (apart from having that brilliantly kinked mental gene that enabled them to take a punt on £20 million and come out in front) who liked to get pissed and swear their faces off and cause a commotion in the streets: but the sheer labour that paid for it, the long, demented, punishing hours, the *work* – that *dignified* them, made them very nearly *heroic*. Here they were, doing something that most of us could never do, and doing it with the most awful, terrible, *commitment* – because that was the only way you could do that particular job – and they were like the Stakhanovites of Las Vegas.

Sharedealing goes hi-tech in Richard Rogers' Diamond-Dogs' look Lloyds Building.

Class and money – the old fixations, but given a wonderful new twist. Because if the City's class nightmare got you interested, the money, the beautiful product of this nightmare, was absolutely riveting. First of all, you could admit that money was the be-all of life: *at last you could say it*. And secondly, you could see that vast quantities of money and vast quantities of work not only went together like ham and eggs, but were suddenly better than sex. And you understood: this was what America had been on about all those years. If you worked hard and made what looked like an absolute fortune, you felt good about it. And if, in sordid, run-down Britain, there was some way you could work hard and make a packet, then a new world of possibilities opened up around you. Of course, Mrs Thatcher had been expatiating on every citizen's duty to toil away and be productive and make a good living for one's dependents, but that sounded like no more than a headmistressy way of telling you to do your best on sports day. No, this City stuff: this was the proof, the reality behind the flannel.

Religion And The Rise Of Capitalism, Part II

Work had always been good though. There may not have been much Protestant work ethic left in the UK by 1980, but there was enough to revive the connection between goodness and labour, the inherent worth of hard work. Add to that the prospect of some serious rewards for your hard work and it wasn't hard to conflate all the terms of the sum and simply conclude that if work was good and work equalled money, then money was good… Provided you'd, well, *worked for it.*

What a strange sensation… telling someone you'd been up all night working and making it sound sexier than telling them you'd been up all night having sex… talking in graphic terms (terms which would have been *offensive* five years earlier) about exactly how much things were *worth* and what your economic worth (as an individual economic unit) was… having to zip about town in what were clearly your *work clothes* because you were the kind of person who had lots of (hugely well-paid) *work* to do… It was no wonder that schoolkids and university students were disgusting and appalling their middle-aged product-of-the-welfare-state professors by getting their exam passes and carefully reading up all the promotional recruitment literature from Salomon Brothers and Kleinwort Benson….

If there was one tiny residual problem with the City as an object of adoration, it was that, even allowing for the press coverage generated by Big Bang and the years of salary explosion that had preceded it, the City still loved the principle of anonymity. It had to: if you wanted to launch a take-over bid worth £150 million on some unsuspecting company, you didn't want to do it in the company of a bunch of loudmouths and media darlings. You wanted lawyers who kept their lips zipped and merchant bankers who smiled and burnished their pinky rings and charmed any unwanted interference clean out of the door.

Local Difficulties

When City people did get their faces around, it was usually for the wrong reasons. Christopher Heath, for instance, was an assiduous director of Baring Securities (part of what used to be Baring Bros of late memory), a quiet, hard-working fellow, who also happened to be Britain's highest-salaried person, earning over £2.5 million a year. It was a bit of a surprise to him when the hounds of the press started breaking down his front door to find out exactly what such a rare creature could look like. It was also bad for business. Part of his job was to have no face. You couldn't make deals if everyone kept asking about your latest appearance in the *Daily Mail*: it made you sound like Dai Llewellyn, when you were supposed to be discreetly manoeuvring someone through the Hang Seng. But there were worse ways to get famous.

The merchant bank Morgan Grenfell – up to the mid-eighties usually considered a bit thrusting – got all the press coverage anyone could want, when at the end of 1986, Geoffrey Collier was done for insider dealing. He went from being head of securities business at MG (with an income of, say, £250 000 a year) to expulsion from the Stock Exchange, a suspended prison sentence and a £25 000 fine at the Old Bailey. The tabloids completely devoured him and his family, because, even though we envied and admired the guys who were making a killing out of killing themselves, journalists love bad apples. But even Collier had to yield pride of place to his colleague, Roger Seelig, when it seemed Seelig was had up.

And Seelig, of course, came to the light as part of the Distillers take-over bid, initiated by 'Deadly' Ernest Saunders, Guinness' CEO at the time. Well, there was a lot of stuff about illicit share support operations, with Morgan Grenfell at the centre of it all and half-a-dozen top City people and modern capitalists involved, and it all took a long time to sort out… but the story broke at the start of 1987 and by autumn of the same year, Seelig had been arrested. *Bad publicity*… because not only did it hammer Morgan Grenfell, not only did it come straight after Collier, but worst of all, it showed the world what a City princeling (which Seelig undoubtedly was) actually looked like. And he looked *bizarre*: he had this awkward, ramrod posture, this apparently lacquered, almost armoured hair, and this peculiarly twisted smile that came out as a kind of Victorian despot's sneer.

From the City point of view, it looked as if Seelig had blown it because he was charged (though subsequently acquitted) and had had to go public, losing the anonymity which was every City banker's *sine qua non*. From the Public point of view, Seelig appeared as something out of a painting by the Victorian artist Sir William Quiller Orchardson, both formal and unfathomable.

Clearly, the City was only going to work as a dream factory within certain very limited parameters. It had the money, but it wasn't going to provide the celebrities, a new plutocracy to lead us forward into the world of money possibilities. The City provided generic types – braying twenty-six-year-olds in stripey shirts and big braces; patrician moneybags with Eton and Winchester educations; thugs in white socks; a few, sparse City Women, with rectilinear suits and don't-fuck-with-*me* expressions – rather than individual characters. This was one reason why it leant itself so well to broad-brush satirical stuff like *Serious Money*, where we were dealing with Jonsonian grotesques, rather than individuals with hopes and fears and feelings. It was in the nature of the beast. Fortunately, however, help was at hand, and from a completely unexpected source: British business.

Lord Stokes And The Charisma Deficit

Let's go back to your childhood. Who, on earth, was running Britain's Great Enterprises, back in the seventies? Hard to remember, isn't it? Back in the seventies, British business was still in that large, grey, lumpen, featureless, unimpressive condition which had become so much a condition of the known world at the time, that it was hard to imagine any large British concern which didn't resemble an ocean of cement, slowly setting. And the boss figures did nothing to alter this view.

Take Lord Stokes, at the head of British Leyland, forever puzzling over fresh reports and commissions and enquiries, trying to drag together the disparate ambitions of the unions, his senior managers and the British government. Poor old Stokes kept popping up on TV, looking old and irascible and worn-out – like Sir Monty Finniston, his equivalent at the British Steel Corporation, another nationalized dinosaur, lumbering helplessly from the late nineteenth to the late twentieth century, wallowing from one collapse to another. Lord Stokes was hardly the sort of man whose 'lifestyle' – to insert a gross anachronism – would arouse any curiosity. We didn't remotely want to know about Lady Stokes' wardrobe, or Bobby Stokes or Chateau Stokes. Even Michael Edwardes, tipped as an industrial go-getter, a man to sort out the unions, who took over at Leyland from Stokes, started off short, pugnacious, and sharp and clearly in the mood for blood, but ended up only just in time to avoid that Royal commission farce.

Even successful businessmen, like Lord Weinstock, hardly made you sit up and take notice. In the bunkered climate of the seventies, the more characterless and corporate the boss figure appeared, the happier everyone seemed to be. And as for entrepreneurs

– guys who dared to do it, who *risked it all*, to make themselves rich and incidentally bring extra life to the Gross Domestic Product – they didn't exist. Or rather they existed in the US and in American movies, where that kind of virile self-realization remained too central to the American Way to die. And they existed, too, in Britain's folkloric past, in the forms of great nineteenth-century capitalists like Armstrong and Cubitt.

The Business Celebrity Generation

Yet, miraculously, the eighties threw up a binload of entrepreneurial British business-men who not only kept their shareholders happy for, well, *years* – they also became objects of fascination in their own right – semi-stars, the missing links between the furtively filthy riches of the City, and the supressed yearning the British had nurtured all those years, for men of destiny. That great pantheon of names: King, Sugar, Maxwell, Halpern, Ronson, Ratner, Hanson, Branson and Conran – men who man-aged the unimaginable feat of getting off the business pages and onto the diary pages, who made the business pages like news pages – big pix, big headlines – and who got profiled more times in the space of five years than their predecessors had in twenty-five.

And what a rich variety there was to choose from! Hairy men, smooth men, young movers and shakers, oldsters who'd suddenly peaked in the eighties, suave NW1ers who'd gone Stock Market-a-go-go, rough diamonds, sharkish survivors who came out to bask in the warm sunshine of the Nation's approval….

And Alan Sugar became a hero. *Incredible.* There he was, this short, scowling, sole-trader type, brought up in a flat in Hackney, his face permanently creased in a frown of belligerence or sus-picion, decorated with a kind of *door-*

Alan Sugar and Rupert Murdoch share a dream.

INTERVIEW

TIM LEFROY

Advertising Agent for the

British Gas Privatization

Q Tim, what was your brief for the British Gas privatization, what did you have to do?

A We had to get in excess of three million shareholders.

Q How did you go about it?

A Well the process of planning the advertising campaign was to understand the start point, what the mentality of potential investors was. We were looking for a lot of people who had no concept of owning shares, who didn't know how to go about it, who didn't know what it would mean to them, and all of that started to emerge from market research... There'd only been one large privatization before – that of British Telecom. That had created a great deal of interest and a lot of people had made, apparently, a quick killing and so the concept of privatization was established,.

Q So you had to get a lot of people off the mark actually into the shop, so to speak, buying shares very quickly.

A Oh, yes. The overall process of building the image of the company as a worthy prospect for investment started in around January 1986, but the actual flotation campaign didn't start until the beginning of September, and the shares were on the market at the beginning of December.

Q Who did your brief for the privatization advertising actually come from, who was your client?

A This was one of the intriguing parts of the process, because of course the client was manifest in very many forms. The primary client was the Department of Energy, jointly with the Treasury, but of course the Central Office of Information was the commissioning agent for all advertising agencies and then we had the merchant back, Rothschild's, and we had of course the company itself British Gas.

Q The Treasury wanted to raise, what was it £5 billion?

A Something in that region.

Q So that was a pretty urgent objective, but were there other objectives there?

A Well, I think a lot of people would say that there may have been a social engineering objective, popular capitalism.

Q Getting ordinary people into the vision of the stock market, popular capitalism, owning a stake in it. So when you got down to the job how did you reckon you had to do it? What did your research show?

A Our research showed that the vast majority of the UK population were either unaware or disinterested in the concept of owning shares... There were only just over two and a half million shareholders in the United Kingdom, but in those days we had to get many many more than that and so we had to create a sense of movement.

Q How did you do it?

A First thing to do was to understand the phases through which we had to take people. First of all, they couldn't possibly get involved if they weren't aware that the event was coming... Then, of course, the next stage was to put the timing onto the process and to tell them when the event was going to happen.

Q How did Sid come into the picture?

A Sid came into the picture in reality at the end of the awareness phase. We actually started the campaign with Jubilee beacons and gas flames being lit all around the coast of Britain... We were looking for an idea that would allow us to present the picture of the people of Britain passing the news and we were looking for a big advertising idea. In fact, it was the creation of two very clever people, Jeanie Willis and Trevor Melvin. We worked long and hard trying to get the big idea, it was a long time in coming... Eventually into my office they came one day and said here's this idea, not just Sid, but if you see Sid tell him...

Q So you could imagine him any which way you wanted.

A Yes indeed and we did bring him into the picture right at the end of the campaign, but you never actually saw his face.

Q So you had to sell Sid, but who was Sid?

A Who is Sid? Sid is everybody's friend, everybody's friend in the United Kingdom. Somebody you all know.

Q So you came up with the Sid idea, and you went and saw all these terribly nobby people, who were your collective client.

A Yes.

Q What was that like?

A It was very funny. There we were, the ad men more associated with selling baked beans, riding into the walnut-panelled board room of the merchant bank and meeting all the great and the good.

Q This was what, Rothschild's?

A This was Rothschild's, and meeting the steering group there, and presenting this marvellous Sid campaign that we thought was the solution to all their problems. And when we'd done this, there was a pregnant silence, everything stopped... and somebody broke the ice. He said maybe it would be helpful then if I explained at this point. Wasn't it right to say that at least 50 per cent of the people we were advertising to were intellectually bankrupt in any event.

Q To which you said?

A Well, I really didn't know whether to be shocked or horrified, but it did get the conversation rolling... The fact that it went on to be a great success is now a matter of history, but I think it was a coming together of two industries – the great institution of the City and the advertising agent – which somehow was a first, certainly a first for us.

Q Did you advance the cause of popular capitalism do you think?

A Inevitably, because we, brought 2.2 million new shareholders into being.

Q Two point two million new shareholders at a time when the total number of shareholders was what?

A Two point eight.

Q So you practically doubled the shareholding base of the UK?

A Indeed.

Q And what's happened to those people? Are they still Sids, are they still with BG? Are they happy with their shareholding, what do you think?

A A large proportion of them are still with BG, many have subsequently bought electricity companies and become involved in the other privatizations that the government has done.

mat of beard, flogging pile-'em-high-and-sell-'em-cheap stereos, this Essex basic type was a folk hero by 1985. He was Thatcherite, free-marketeering, New Age Venture Opportunity Capitalism made flesh. He spotted gaps in the market and filled them with cheap Amstrad gear, made wherever it was, that everyone bought. Small-scale professionals and freelance hacks and retired civil servants got into the computer age for the first time in their lives with an Amstrad PCW and they loved him for it. Before Sugar brought out the PCW 8256 in 1985, word processor sales in the UK were around 65 000 units a year. Amstrad flogged 350 000 PCWs in the first eight months of sales.

And they loved him because he hated the City but wanted to be rich, just like them; and they loved him because, just like them, he cussed his head off when he felt like it. Sugar describes what he felt when he first saw the instruction manual for the PCW, 'I thought to myself, "There's no *bloody* way a mug like myself would know how to use this." It assumed that people knew about high density disks and formatting disks and all that *cobblers*.' Legends stuck to him, like the time when he was going for Stock Market flotation in 1979 and met the head of Greenwells, the gents' broking firm which was going to handle the placing. Pip Greenwell (the Boss) was late for their first meeting and said, in his cut-glass City voice, 'I'm so terribly sorry we're late, but the *fucking* traffic was awful.' And Sugar stuck out his hand and unzipped the wolfish Sugar grin and said, 'Thank God someone in the City speaks my sort of language.' Yes! *A real guy!* And the symbolism was so poignant, too, the way in which the true eighties were prefigured in this meeting of the old City with the young pretender, both of them joined in an honest, manly desire to make a stack of cash.

The investors loved him as well – for a long time, anyway. When the company was first floated, shares were around the 90p mark, By 1981, they had doubled in value. By late 1982, they were up to 395p for a brief surge of madness, then stayed pretty steady around 300p for the next few years. This was the stuff that made the Winchester-educated city analysts *and* the penny-share investors in their South Coast retirement bungalows feel good all over. Sugar even survived being made the *Guardian*'s Young Businessman of the Year in 1984. The hype was *good*. It wasn't just Sugar banging about making a lot of blue noise at AGMs, it was proof that the human dynamo who *was* Amstrad's big success, was still cutting it and making it happen. *You had to have a celebrity chairman....*

The trick could be turned in other ways, too. Look at Terence Conran, for instance. There he was, design guru to a generation of people with flats in Belsize Park and self-renovated workers' cottages in Hammersmith – *Observer* people, fruit and veg-eaters – and he'd given them all the paper lampshades and canvas director's chairs they could possibly want and he was, well, he was fifty years old by this time and he'd opened his first Habitat way back in 1964 and he was very charming and comfortable-looking – really, he looked more like the kind of civilized person who'd be quite happy to let himself be munificently bought out of his own business by some slavering conglomerate in the take-over madness of the early-mid eighties. *But he didn't*: he floated

The look of a man who made it through the decade (and the previous two). Sir Terence Conran's transformation in the eighties to full-scale, full-finance Plc evangelist was one of the most impressive magic tricks of the age. At last an entrepreneur for us, Tamsin.

Habitat on the Stock Market in 1980 (giving himself a holding valued at £25 million at the time), then took over Mothercare in 1982 and Richard Shops in 1983, the whole thing winding up in the vast Storehouse PLC, in 1986 (let's not worry too much about the way everything started to fall apart by 1989: it felt great to see someone like him in there, pitching, as it were).

A transfiguring experience: the apotheosis of seventies retailing becomes the civilized end – the Francophile, charmingly-suited end – of the eighties plutocracy. *Another character in the cast* – this time, covering the NW1 realm of financial aspiration (so *right* of him to get involved in Mothercare, you thought at the time, a financial heavyweight who nonetheless would *care* about the shape of a baby's wee feeding bottle). If Sir Terence couldn't make the money-go-round seem justifiable, no one could.

Again, it wasn't simply a question of making the new world of Thatcherite economic possibilities OK with the herbivore class. It, too, was part of the need for a Celebrity Chairman to keep the City cheerful. The old trend for grey men in thick specs was now so completely reversed that if you didn't have a guy at the head who could keep the Business gossip pages supplied with copy and photo opportunities then the investors (who were now getting very American, by the way, looking for a fresh Iacocca at every turn) would conclude that yours was an Uninteresting Investment Opportunity and move their money into something a little more energetic.

Another extreme was Lord King of British Airways. Unlike Conran (the archetypal Smooth Man), King was a hairy Man, but not nearly as Hairy as Alan Sugar. King was actually in his sixties when he became Chairman of BA in 1980, and already had a career behind him in engineering. He was, in fact, the ball bearing king, having run Pollards Ball Bearings very successfully prior to joining BA, and too smoothed out and Establishment-seeming to be a Sugar. But like Sugar, his crowning age was the eighties, by a mile; and like Sugar, he did it by giving the impression that he was wrestling his business problems to the ground and then stamping on their heads. This was the time when he fought the unions and won, turned a national embarrassment into a world-beater, got the business to a stage where it could show a £250 million annual profit without too much pain and where the government could privatize it with all the panache of an alchemist turning a British Rail sandwich into pure platinum.

When BA went on the market in February 1987, the amount on offer was £223 million: the offer was over-subscribed thirty-five times – there was £8 billion chasing the issue. And when they hit the floor, the 65p part-paid shares immediately started trading at 119p. And Lord King did it – this tough, beady old fighter with the prodding forefinger and the build of someone who's passed through a car-crusher *and survived*, this man who had made it happen for the cheering investors of Britain – he was the apotheosis of the chairman. As long as King was there, larger than life, acting the part, then BA could make it and the City and the private investors (who'd been dragged in by the irresistible suction of cheap privatization issues) would be happy.

It didn't stop there, though. On the one hand, there was Lord King, the epitome of the New Business Age, raising Lazarus from the dead and conjuring money out of the ether. On the other hand, there was Lord King as a very rich man, with an annual salary of around £1 million (part from BA, part from Babcock International, the engineering company of which he was *also* chairman), owning a place in Eaton Square, a country house with 2000 acres in Leicestershire and another in Scotland, and master of the Belvoir Hunt. Lord King, was, in short, a real, traditional, rather nineteenth-century style plutocrat and part of his success was precisely this – that he did the business and reaped the rewards. He looked the part *and* he helped feed the new chroniclers of wealth, the features and society people who had to fill up the proliferating soft news pages and colour mags. He was an object of straightforward envy and admiration. Particularly since, so it turned out, he'd made it from nowhere.

An Example To Us All

It didn't get as bad as *Lifestyles Of The Rich And Famous* here, mind you, but it was all part of the process of *describing* the world of wealth to an admiring public lingering on the details – the sort of thing that Tom Wolfe has called Plutography, the depiction of hidden acts of wealthiness. Of course, this has always been around in one modest archaic form or another in this country – whether it's been sneaking a peek at Lady Docker's latest gold-plated Daimler or Lord Berners' multi-coloured doves and the piano in the back of his Rolls-Royce, or even in Bill Brandt's classic photographs of the rich in between-wars London. The difference between eighties Plutography and all that was that the eighties' version was infinitely brassier – more intrusive (and what's in *this* little room?) and far more interested in price tags and net worth. The reader was looking for 'role models', and interior decoration hints. He wasn't deferential. The *Telegraph Magazine* pointed out this change nicely one week in 1987, when it ran a profile of a smart, pearl-roped lady who judged etiquette matters; but preceded that typically *Telegraph* item with a double page spread entitled 'You'll Be Amazed What Money Can Buy' – including a shoot with Captain Mark Phillips (£1200) and a photograph with Charles and Diana (£30 000).

In other words, that old-time correctitude was all very useful, but now the readers wanted to get where the smart set were – and they knew they could *because everything had a price*. And when we watched *Dallas* and *Dynasty*, we did it in a very strange frame of mind: part of us was wallowing in the old British irony and laughing at these gross cartoons; part of us was silently envious (nice poolside scenes; delicious scale and comfort, however livid); and a small but not insignificant part of us was taking notes towards a future life of absolute wealth – a life which one day, just possibly, we might know. And not a few girls noticed Alexis' business ploys as well as her shoulder pads.

In this climate of uncritical fascination, celebrity bosses had to be seen to be doing the things that rich people did. So Lord King – who 'came from absolutely nothing' as a friend put it, just to add an extra shine to legend – was photographed as master of the Belvoir Hunt. Gerald Ronson, owner of the Heron Corporation, Britain's second largest private company, was not only known to be sitting on a personal fortune of between £700 million and £1 billion (before his awkward involvement with Guinness, this is) but also had to be seen out and about, with his wife – 'glamorous ex-model Gail', as the tabloids always called her – to charity fund-raisers larded with the Great and the Good and the Rich and Famous.

Gerald Ratner, the man who took the rather low-profile family jewellery firm and turned it into Ratners Plc, the Stock Market favourite (with 1700 shops throughout the UK) appeared in *ES* magazine, the London *Evening Standard*'s glossy colour supp, not to talk about his p/e ratio or his expansion plans, but as a plutocrat in a piece about powerful businessmen needing *at least* three secretaries. At the time, he was feeling pretty good about life; he'd taken the loss-making business in 1984, worked for the next five years, getting it to turn in a £121 million profit by the end of the decade. He had huge offices just off Berkeley Square, a late nineteenth-century robber baron's London house from the look of it, and there he was, photographed with his three marvellous secretaries, arranged around his immense desk, with a portrait of... the Duke Of Marlborough? Wellington? on the wall behind him. Images of power... plutography.

Business magazine, launched in 1986 by Kevin Kelly, inventor of *Interiors*, was a pure high-gloss plutography medium from the start, regularly devoting itself to full-colour profiles of big-timers and Up and Comings in finance and commerce, turning itself into the Stock Market's own *Interiors* on the way. Even someone like Peter Earl (a small-time merchant banker and City *enfant terrible*, who kept attempting incredibly audacious things like the take-over of Storehouse) got the full *Business* treatment, complete with wife, kids and super yellow Sloane Street family house.

Tom Wolfe himself became a kind of plutographer when he produced *The Bonfire Of The Vanities*: a Wall Street novel which seemed so intimate, so privy to its subjects and their fabulously rich lives that it looked sometimes like an act of veneration rather than desecration. Look at this! Even *Serious Money* celebrated the awful cash-crazy, hedonistic vitality of the people it was supposed to be crucifying. (I got up an office party to see it, idiotically expecting the audience to be full of ditch-the-bitch types in black denim. But of course all my bright eyed colleagues were thrilled to see all their little friends from Kleinwort Benson and Morgan Grenfell and so on. It couldn't have been more social.)

All the same, there were times when the public gaze got a little *too* intense and the celebrity plutocrats got a little *carried away* with their performances. To pluck a name at random: Sir Ralph Halpern was, without a doubt, a good thing for the Burton Group. He'd worked his way up (wonderful when that happens, always a sign of real character) from nowhere – a job with Montagu Burton in Leeds in the early sixties – to being head of a £2 billion clothing and retail conglomerate including Burtons, Top Shop and Debenhams. And he was paid around £1 million a year.

All of which was fine and much welcomed by the shareholders, notwithstanding a few off-the-record observations about Halpern's somewhat *showbiz* approach to things, which eventually included a topless model called Fiona Wright and a lot of very untechnical stuff about five-times-a-night sex and Sir Ralph being 'Bonking Barmy', as the tabloids had it. Now, there he was, this rich, powerful and successful man misbehaving and cheating on his wife – *the absolute image of a moneyed fat cat* – and yet he was instantly forgiven – more than that, he went feet first into legend. A generation earlier, he'd have been caricatured in *OZ* magazine. But *now*, in this new climate, he could even use his lapses to advantage: at the next AGM after all his tabloid excursions, instead of hiding behind his name card and getting his colleagues to do all the talking, he came out fighting and faced his critics down. What a man! Tiger stuff!

And it was *all* good for the great cast of characters. It rounded them out very nicely. You had a good spread of identifiable talents, personalities and behavioural quirks, the greatest soap of all by the second half of the eighties. Just right for keeping everyone's interest on the boil.

Filling The Gap

But it did more than that. The effect started to trickle down, to borrow a popular phrase of the time. For some people – well, a large number, judging by the way they filled the nation's consciousness at the time – it wasn't enough just to watch the great play of characters in the business and social pages. For some people, it was more important than that: *they had to do it themselves.* They had to start their own businesses.

It was a world full of possibilities. Not only were there opportunities (down South, at least) in all those modern service businesses like finance and marketing and estate agency; there was, the mythology of 'spotting the gap' which needed to be filled by some bright, hard-working entrepreneur. There were niches wherever you looked: clothes ironing services, corporate art advisory services, home-watching services for hectic executives who were always out of the country, caterers for the yuppie class and itinerant fresh sandwich merchants, darting among the dealers' pens like little fish among the rocks. And they were all entrepreneurs, all buying a tiny piece of whatever it was that had got Lord Hanson (another Great Player, the Vulpine One) going, a quarter of a century earlier. You name it and they'd give it a try; although to be honest, they weren't really dreaming about a little Hanson Trust of their own when they turned off the light after a hard day's flogging sandwiches or pressing Bond Dealers' shirts. They were dreaming about Sophie Mirman.

The Millionairess Next Door

For a brief but beautiful time, Sophie Mirman was the patron saint of the little entrepreneurs. Everyone knew her story and everyone held it up to the light and fiddled around with it and worried over it, trying to see how they could get a little of it. Sophie had started a little boutique in Knightsbridge Underground Station, early in the eighties, from which she sold socks and stockings – hosiery. Nothing else, just hosiery. It was called the Sock Shop. It was so simple, so uncluttered, it was hard to see, at first, what was the *point* of it. But Sophie (who had borrowed £45 000 on a government Loan Guarantee Scheme to start it up) persevered. And by 1988 she had 61 shops in the UK and three in New York and sales of over £14 million a year. And she was only just 30.

Even more hypnotically gripping: she had taken Sock Shop onto the USM – the Unlisted Securities Market, a smaller, higher-risk mini-Stock Exchange for young businesses, 'Entrepreneurial, fast growing and *sexy*,' as one USM prophet put it – initially punting the shares at 125p. The issue was oversubscribed fifty-four times and shares started trading at 205p, giving the the company a value of £60 million… all this from one little retail chancer in an Underground Station started by a girl whose working career, so it is said, had originally been in the typing pool at Marks & Spencer (the reality of her background was rather less modest than this). In early 1988, she was voted USM Entrepreneur of the Year and in late 1988, she was voted Businesswoman of the Year. If there was ever a way of doing things, then this, surely, was it.

It all came to grief a year later, but she had at least done *all that*, she'd shown that it was *possible*. So then, quite suddenly, there seemed to be hundreds of people up and down the country, saying things like, 'I'm thinking of starting a little business,' and then telling you about the long hours spent hugger-mugger with the accountants and the bank manager and the colleagues who were going into the same little business with them. The most astonishing middle-manager 'lifers' started doing it (particularly when it looked as if their jobs wouldn't be there for long). And for the first time in many people's lives, things were *genuinely exciting*: destiny called – and everyone could be his – or her – own Sophie Mirman – or even his own Roy Bishko, Chairman of Tie Rack, the franchise company which had taken on the job of accessorizing the torso (ties, ornamental hankies, cravats) and by 1988 was turning in profits of £2.66 million, on sales from 165 outlets.

On Your Bike

There was this feeling of *Men – You Can Do It*, egged on by the government (promoting publications like the *Small Business Action Kit*), by the Press (which took this frenzied activity to be a popular thing to run with – 'Getting Down To Business – The Earlier The Better; No Business Like Small Business' and so on), and, naturally, the banks. The banks actually hit new highs of sanctimonious baloney, about putting your trust in their small business advisers who were there, like something out of a Whitney

Houston number, to catch you when you fell and put you back on your feet again, and were forever shown, smiling and nodding and encouraging an assortment of wild-eyed packaging designers, sheep farmers, silage exporters and stonemasons.

And if you didn't want to do the whole thing yourself – find a market, do your own letterheads, get the VAT sorted out and deal with the million other non-visionary aspects to business – you could get into a *franchise*. The perfect eighties small business *entree*, anything from carpet-cleaning to travel agencies to splattergun executive war games to McDonalds… to Tie Rack… Roy Bishko actually claimed that he wanted to turn Tie Rack into 'the McDonalds of the clothing business'.

Be a small businessman overnight! Get a load of ties from Tie Rack and learn from

Where big business and environmentally friendly products could peacefuly co-exist – the Body Shop was conviction merchandising to the max.

The commodity gets style and makes millions: Phileas Fogg stakes a claim on our feelings and on every drinks party.

the inside! Or go into interior design and work it all out for yourself! You can do it! Small businesses were *everywhere* – and in the Great Chain Of Being, they led all the way from the highest points of the City Of London, via the Great Players with their incredible lives and incredible fortunes, through the Little Entrepreneurs who hit pay-dirt, all the way down to the men with brilliant new schemes for cleaning the windows of the small offices where the small businessmen were setting up their small, over-borrowed businesses in a mood of exhilaration and dread.

The Great Chain Of Being: an unbroken line of cash, chance, hope, fear and bright ideas… It was wonderful. It united us all, in a true and unforced love of Money.

It made the point – if the point hadn't been made before – that from now on, we were *Americans.* The UK, having gone through all kinds of tortures and miseries and reversals, was now stabilizing in a way which would have seemed wholly unlikely twenty years before, but which now made perfect sense. After all, we had two leaders with essentially the same worldview; we had the same Anglo-Saxon economic casino system of finance and reward; we had the same booming service and finance industries, the same declining manufacturing industries – the 'rust belt', the same decadent fascination in the production values.

In Britain, we even had a prime minister who, for once, was *admired* by an American president. Did it matter that much that he was mentally neither here nor there? Not that much, when he got the USA to start making favourable comparisons

Medomsley Rd. Consett.

between Mrs T. and Churchill. It was euphoric, it was like the Royal Wedding or the Falklands – did you have a moment's pause about it all? After that, the pleasure took over again and the euphoria swept us on. We had the same collective political leadership. We bought the same CDs and we watched the same movies and we all hung on *Dynasty* with our senses burning. The cultural love affair which had got us all silly over things like inter-state advertising hoardings and milkshakes and bizarre slacks and the Grand Canyon and Times Square had come to a climax.

But unlike the surface stuff – the way we'd loved their vulgarity and they loved our nineteenth-century stuffiness – this was altogether deeper, altogether a more *structural thing.* We were in this one *together.* And when Gordon Gekko, in *Wall Street,* came out with that stuff about 'Greed clarifies, greed cuts through and captures the essence of the evolutionary spirit…' – and gets you Kim Basinger – on both sides of the Atlantic the Anglo-Saxon, market-driven, cash-hungry audiences looked and listened and tut-tutted along with Oliver Stone's heavy-handed satire – but in their darkest, most secret souls, they were saying… *Yes.…*

P U S H E R S

Let's start at the top and work our way down. In September 1987, Saatchi & Saatchi, the world's largest advertising agency at the time, decided it was going to buy the Midland Bank. Yes, the Midland Bank, one of the big four High Street banks, a national institution of sorts, thirty years earlier the biggest bank *in the world*, the Listening Bank, *that* Midland Bank. And Saatchi & Saatchi, an ad agency seemingly staffed by advertising ponces, eternally cheerful men with big glasses and floppy bow ties, and women with immense padded shoulders and permanent scowls – walking Heath jokes, all of them in the persistent view of most regular business folk – *these people* were going to appropriate a huge piece of the nation's financial infrastructure and run it as a going concern. What larks! *Hilarious.* Like something out of Tom Sharpe. Or The Marx Brothers.

The big window for the big agency – Saatchis had a view on a bigger world, the City, government... herself.

Real Business

But they meant it. They were *serious*. The way the Saatchi brothers looked at it, they saw themselves running a huge, multinational corporation which employed over 14 000 people around the world, which was well-known on the Stock Exchange (it had been listed for over a decade by this time) and was much approved by the brokers and analysts, and which could (and did) turn in regular, large profits. In 1986, these profits had gone up 73 per cent, to £70 million. In 1987, they went up again, this time by 77 per cent, to £124 million. Earnings per share and dividends per share both went up by 20 per cent. *Serious performance*: there was no doubting it.

The Midland, on the other hand, was now so far from being the biggest bank in the world that it didn't even make it into the world's top twenty. It was the smallest of the big four in the High Street; it had recently got itself into a terrible state with a load of bad South American debts; and it had tried to expand into the United States by taking over the Crocker Bank of California, with the predictable consequences that Crocker had turned out to be a loser and they'd had to get rid of it fast.

By 1987, the Midland had had to make a £1 billion provision against its Third World loans and had had to sell off two of its subsidiary banks, the Northern and the Clydesdale. And having set up Greenwell Montagu as its toehold in the big bad world of the post-Bang City, it found, at the start of 1987, that Greenwell Montagu was losing a mass of money on the market-making side: so it closed the market-making operation at a loss of £6 million. At the time, everything the Midland did seemed shot through with the purest eighties exorbitance; on top of which, it had saddled itself in its promotional gear with a cartoon griffin, which popped out, smirking at customers whenever they came in to collect their cash. On this count alone, the Midland was not an entirely *serious* bank.

So the Saatchis decided, this is the way forward: *the multi-service business*. Get it all under one roof – advertising, marketing, management consultancy… *finance*. They'd already bought up these other bits from all over the world, why not add the fourth? Why not get a bank? Think total service: in comes the client through one door, picking up all the creative and intellectual skills he needs (no need to shop around, now) and out he goes through the other door, clutching not only a load of marketing strategies, made-to-measure advertising and business plans, but a fat cheque to spend on the whole thing, courtesy of the Saatchis' very own bank. *That's how people thought in those days.*

Could they afford it? Well, Saatchis were valued on the Stock Market at a bit less than £1 billion. Midland was capitalized on the Stock Market at £2 billion. Saatchis would have to pay well over the odds to buy the bank, so that meant paying about £3 billion. Then they'd have to offer some extra cash to keep everyone happy and top up the bank's finances. In other words, the ad people would have to have access to £4 billion, mainly by raising funds on the Stock Market. But in those days… £4 billion? It was OK. It was fine. The Saatchis had so much power that no one even broke into a sweat at the prospect of that kind of money.

Then Sir Kit McMahon, Chairman of Midland Bank said, what if you had to raise another £1 billion, to bale out a load of Latin Americans? It could happen. So the Saatchis paled somewhat and then McMahon told his board about the proposition and the board agreed that it wouldn't be the thing at all to be taken over by a load of admen and the Saatchis left, to try and buy a City merchant bank called Hill Samuel. Which went fine for a few days, until the rest of the world found out that Saatchis had tried to buy the Midland. And then the rest of the world began saying things like, 'The Saatchis have run out of ideas' and they were 'megalomaniacs' and were 'carried away by their own self-importance'… and the price of Saatchi shares slipped fairly heavily on the Stock Exchange and as a result they couldn't afford to buy Hill Samuel either. And then the October Stock Market crash came and knocked about a third off the value of the agency's shares and that was the end of the Saatchis' financial ambitions….

The Voodoo Arts

Of course it was: this was the advertising world, the world of the Voodoo Arts – *half of all advertising is a waste of money, but you can never tell which half* – a world populated by hucksters and deranged, semi-creative animals. This was a world which was a bit like the world of the City, with its very large salaries and its flash cars and its stunning pretensions; but it was much, much smaller and much, much sillier.

This was a world where the tone was set by *Campaign*, the magazine for everyday advertising folk. *Campaign* at around this time was deliberately and persistently crazy in the way it dealt with advertising news – BUNGEY MEDICAL UNIT SCOOPS DRUG DOUBLE, it would holler; or BARTLE BOGLE WINS KUDOS IN 'BADA' RACE; or BOASE IN 3M BEER BLITZ – these huge, insane headlines would come plunging out of the magazine, every one accompanied by a doom-laden black and white photo of some stricken account director in the corner of a *Citizen Kane*-sized office. Hilarious stuff, and the ad boys and girls loved it. But it was silly, just like the business, where people spent millions of pounds and their entire working lives on George the Hofmeister Bear and Captain Birdseye. *Ridiculous stuff.*

And yet… and yet it was a Voodoo Art the British actually did quite well. Strange – but while the old dark, reeky industries of coal, steel, car making and engineering and so forth were going through nightmares of downsizing, restructuring and disintegration, the Voodoo Arts were really coming along very nicely. It was something we were good at; and there was a lot of talk at the time of how we were all going to turn our backs on the old manufacturing principles of the nineteenth century and become a fully-integrated, post-industrial service economy, bringing brain skills, marketing and finance to the rest of the world, while the rest of the world dully plugged away at making *stuff.* The service economy was going to power us through to the next Golden Age of Western Capitalism. And in adland, it really seemed to be happening.

Back to the Saatchis: in the first half of the eighties, they epitomized this splendid new world to the nth degree. They bought up huge numbers of ad agencies, all over the world, and dragged them into the big Saatchi communal tent. Half of Madison Avenue fell to the brothers – agencies like Comptons and Ted Bates and McCaffery & McCall and Backer & Spielvogel and Dancer Fitzgerald Sample – hundreds of millions of dollars' worth of whacky ad agency names – and everyone Stateside started making the joke that SAATCHI was really an acronym for Single Ad Agency Takes Control of Half the Industry, *ha ha.* They also bought businesses outside New York – on the West Coast, in Canada, in Europe, the Far East, Australasia and Britain itself. And they bought up just about anything that moved and could possibly fit into the total plan: advertising, market research, management consultancy, you name it.

Naturally, they had the accounts to go with their ambitions. Very Blue Chip stuff, very prestigious: British Airways, Guinness, Proctor & Gamble – anyone you care to name, virtually. But the account that made Saatchis famous was – for some people – the most Blue Chip of all: the Conservative Party. In the 1979 election, Callaghan had relied on the usual Labour assemblage of volunteers and helpful PR types to get the campaign launched, while the Tories used the Saatchis and their 'Labour Isn't Working' poster, and won the election. Not only did this make Saatchis the only famous ad agency in the country, it made them credible. It made them part of the

TIM MELLORS

Advertising Executive

Q Tim, how did you get into Saatchis?

A I was just approached. I'd actually been directing commercials. And I came to the end of that and, sort of mystically, I was approached by Saatchis, went along, talked to them, and was immediately sucked in.

Q What were you being sucked into? Did you know?

A I was fascinated by it from the outside... for the first time, an adverting agency became a public thing. It was the only advertising that your mum would know the name of.

Q And what was it like once you got inside?

A It wasn't like any other advertising agency I'd ever been in... There was a tremendous competitive edge in the place... Saatchi & Saatchi was all about success, and excess.

Q So communication was hot, Saatchis were famous. What else gave them this terrific self-esteem?

A To me, the heart of the agency was Charles himself. When he was Charlie Saatchi, the copywriter, he was a very clever, witty writer. There was another side of him which was an art collector and art dealer, and... he was behaving more like an art person. So what he was bringing to the agency was a lot of energy in an artistic sense.

Q What would you regard as a really excessive eighties-feeling ad that could never have been before and couldn't be now?

A I think Saatchi and Saatchi made its name basically on two accounts, though it did lots more famous ones... the Conservative Party and British Airways.

Q You were in some way related to that City thing, where there were a lot of young people with money coming our of their ears. How did Saatchis relate to that?

A For a long time [Saatchis] was a very good share. It was something that the City thought was an extremely good option. These great big monolithic companies started to believe that Saatchi & Saatchi could work some magic for them... And there were all these flotations, and Saatchi & Saatchi got a lot of those to do. We became seen as the natural choice for... huge corporate cultures.

Q Being close to the government and to the Tory Party – was that important in the everyday feelings of self-esteem of people in the agency?

A Yes. Of course it was. We were the agency of choice for the government in power... That gave us a specialness.

Q How did it go wrong?

A It started to, in my opinion anyway, go wrong when Tim Bell left the agency... [and] within months Charles and Maurice moved out of the building... The eighties were coming to an end, and therefore as an eighties agency, it had a natural life and it evolved into something different – some would say better, some would say worse. But it wasn't the same.

Establishment. It put an ad agency somewhere up there in the pantheon of Seriously Powerful. It meant that admen could come in from the cold.

Boys On The Big Band

Which they did in large numbers. Saatchis may have been the name everyone knew, but there were a lot of other outfits chasing the same dreams of power, wealth, importance and New Age Voodoo Arts respectability. There were people like Wight Collins Rutherford Scott, who had as its frontman someone called Robin Wight, who talked a lot and wore bow ties and wanted to be a Tory MP and had his face in *Campaign* week in, week out. WCRS started the eighties as a nice little London Loves kind of Terribly Creative agency, but in the space of about five years, had ballooned into a significant international business with a Stock Exchange listing, millions of pounds' worth of acquisitions and profits for 1986 of £10 million.

There was BMP (Boase Massimi Pollitt), who went public, bought up all kinds of desirable operations and turned in profits of £5 million in 1986. There was Lowe Howard Spink, who went public in 1984, bought up some businesses, and made loads of money, and there was Gold Greenlees Trott, which was famous for having a creative director called Dave Trott who looked like a Division Two psycho midfielder and went around shouting at everyone and having his picture in *Campaign*, week in, week out. So they went public in 1985, shares oversubscribed fifty-nine times. As did Abbott Mead Vickers – the same year, same massive oversubscription of shares, led by a Kilroy lookalike called David Abbott whose face was in *Campaign*, week in, week out.…

It was Boom Time in Soho and Covent Garden and Charlotte Street W1 in London. It was Klondike for the purveyors of dreams. Because not only were there these big, rich, powerful ad agencies with their faces in *Campaign* and the money of thousands of shareholders; there were countless other, smaller agencies, some of them very small indeed, doing their best to surf in on the tide of money that was keeping the big ones afloat. In the first half of the decade, people were shifting jobs and scurrying from agency to agency and leaving and starting their own agencies at a bewildering rate. A standard procedure was to establish some kind of presence with a medium-to-large agency, quit, launch your own tiny-but-perfect agency with some other disaffected people, promise to offer uncompromising standards of service to your clients, get your picture plus profile interview in *Campaign* (squeezed in between the Porsche and BMW colour ads) and then wait for another medium-to-large agency to buy you out for cash plus car plus share options.

There was *so* much money around in those golden years… £2 billion spent on advertising in the UK in 1980, up to £5 billion by 1986… who *needed* heavy industry? Who *needed* factories in the Midlands making driveshafts for Austin Rover? Down here, down in London W1, down in Adland, things were altogether richer and nicer and cleaner – a life surrounded by white walls, high windows, pieces of modern art, brightly-coloured marker pens, fig trees in pots, pretty women, cars…

Absolutely Fabulous

… And the effect spread. The Voodoo Arts grew and blossomed. Pretty soon it wasn't just the admen of Soho and Covent Garden who were doing well. All sorts of bizarre Voodoo Arts practices – *un-British* practices – were being financed by all sorts of clients. PR, for instance – *Public Relations* – which, until then, had been a two-way joke: either because it made everyone think of US-style PR which was very loud and obvious and crass and amusing; or because it summoned up visions of old-style British PR, which was for a long time not much more than a loose national assemblage of ex-army and RAF officers who'd been given cushy billets in Unilever and Shell and told to fire off the odd press release and take their hack journalist friends out to Madame Prunier's for a few bottles of Burgundy.

Jokes… Yet in Britain in the eighties, PR went from nothing – from the old boys writing hand-outs – to around £12 million in 1980 in fees for the main members of the Public Relations Consultants' Association, to over £50 million for the same companies in 1985. By 1986, the Shandwick Group alone (Britain's biggest) was taking in over £13 million a year, with the Charles Barker Group second on £7 million. By 1988, PR was being touted as *the fastest growing business sector in the UK* – total revenue had risen by 45 per cent in the preceding 12 months. It became so serious that the business could even support two trade publications – *Public Relations Magazine*, launched in 1982; and *PR Week*, launched in 1984.

Pretty soon, if you were running a business which employed more than three and a half people, you also had a PR firm to project you to the world. Journalists got increasingly used to ringing up tiny little companies for some sort of quote, only to be

INTERVIEW

LYNNE FRANKS

Public Relations Manager

Q How has your life changed since the eighties?

A It's a lot quieter. Well, actually, I'm not sure if that's true. It seems nicer, more peaceful, less frenetic, less chaotic.

Q What was it like in the eighties then?

A Well, I moved so fast that frankly my memories are blurred and it was crazy. I was on the move constantly and just one situation ran into another one before I had even time to be aware of the last one I'd been in. But it was noisy, fun, active.

Q What were the best bits?

A I suppose creating a great launch or just putting lots of different factors together which I did in m job at that point, which was creating excitement and hype around certain things. And knowing that the combination had really gelled and everyone was having fun

Q What were your key things?

A We revised Brylcreem's. Every young man felt that he had to wear some kind of hair gel on his hair to look the part. We put designer labels on bottoms: Gloria Vanderbilt jeans... We were involved in lots of projects. We launched Green Consumer Week: for the first time the consumer became aware that they had power in choosing environmentally friendly products. We worked with Amnesty International on music tours that various artists were doing to create awareness of things like freedom of speech. I was there right in the middle of the British Fashion Industry really getting an international reputation yet again, this time with the help of the newly married Princess Diana and the newly acclaimed Boy George era: that was all happening.

Q What made it all possible to do all those things in the eighties and not really to have been able to do them in the seventies?

A Mmm, there was a lighter, more enthusiastic spirit in the eighties. I always remember decades in colour and for me the seventies were a quite dark decade. The eighties were very colourful to me even though actually if one looks back, there was all the Japanese designer wear and black furniture. But it still seems a very colourful time and people were open to new ideas and there was an optimism in the eighties that wasn't there in the seventies.

Q PR was a profession whose time had come.

A Yes, the PR had always been a sort of younger relative of the advertising industry. It still is to a degree: I mean it's always the smaller budgets. But people started understanding that you could actually sell and reach consumer consciousness on a PR level by promotion – through the media on an editorial basis, by creating excitement around a product.

Q Do you think it was because the papers, the media altogether changed and they wanted PR stuff, they wanted personal stuff, they wanted fashion stuff, instead of wanting hard news stuff?

A Perhaps the fact is there was a more

magaziney type element in the media and therefore magaziney or feature type stories were more appropriate and people had money in their pockets. They were being told that they could earn more, they were worth more because the value of their houses had gone up more. It was all a very optimistic time, so they wanted to know that they could buy, what they could wear, where they could be seen, where they should eat. It was the decade of the yuppies, let's face it.

Q And how come everybody got style? In the seventies, nobody had style.

A Well, because there were all those magazines telling them how to do it. It was do it yourself style, wasn't it? You wear this with this and go here and have this cat and this type of girlfriend and this type of baby accessory, and you've got style.

Q How did you make young people put goo in their hair?

A We created something called the Brylcreem Boy. It was all based on the fact that he not only had to be incredibly good looking but he was also very bright and clever. And we did this search around the countryside at all the trendy clubs, for the Brylcreem Boy and we did all these wonderful graphics, where the last year's boy always looked very smooth and got the girl and dressed in the right stuff, and I think he got the prize as well of modelling contracts. It was when everybody really wanted to be tomorrow's model. It was just by association. It was associating the right thing with the right thing. We were doing

Budweiser for a while and a new programme had just started on TV, so we got the host drinking Budweiser at the end of every show with all his guests. We made sure that all the new Swatches were always sent out to the people that should be wearing them, or the latest pop group and they would go on TV and everybody wanted one – it's all that aspirational selling… The eighties was about dreams and fantasy and fun, it was a different time.

Q When did you first realize that there was a lot of money around? What was the first sort of lesson made you think: God! There's millions to be spent?

A I don't know, it was around, it was evident. The first feeling I ever got that there was more money around was when I saw budgets that we were being given for promotions and for launches… Parties, that's what it was about, lots and lots of parties, wasn't it? I remember lots of parties.

Q How do you feel about PR now?

A It's not something that I wish to spend my time doing any more, because it is changing very rapidly. PR as we know it in the eighties is not going to be around for very much longer: the whole way of communicating is going to change, the whole way of 'marketing' is out of date and obsolete – advertising is not going the same way… I think you're going to find all PR agencies over the next two years are going to drop PR off their names and call themselves Communications Strategy Agencies!

directed by a helpful person in the marketing department to some organization in London W1 which promptly mailed out a whole checklist of fine facts and usable figures and offered to arrange a conversation – usually with the marketing person who'd just redirected them to the PR people. The whole Lynne Franks/AbFab scenario owed its existence to these hothouse days, when PR got shoved on the list of Must Haves, somewhere after the company accountant and before the in-house company caterer. It was like watching mushrooms come up.

PR became a necessity – and Lynne Franks was absolutely fabulous at profile.

The Sainsbury's Synod

And then with PR, you got the rise and rise of *sponsorship*: by the end of the decade, there were over 200 listed sponsorship consultants in the UK. Five years before, there had only been forty. Spending on business sponsorship – cigarette packets on racing cars, washing machines around football pitches, computer company logos on a night at the opera – had reached around £300 million a year and – yes – there was a trade paper, called *Sponsorship News*, a sure sign that things were on the up… a Voodoo Art, indeed, when you couldn't tell what effect your sponsorship budget was having on the minds of the British people or even *if* it was having any effect at all.

When Silk Cut decided to sponsor the Jaguar Motor Racing Team, there was evidently some sort of 're-positioning' of the brand at the back of everyone's mind – take Silk Cut away from being the soft, undemonstrative kind of cigarette that ladies kept in their bags for a quiet puff after dinner; and lend it raw, masculine associations – the noise, the speed, the smell, the hormonal excitement of the race track. Get in there, like Marlboro and Camel and the great grand-daddy of them all, Gold Leaf Team Lotus, back in 1968 – make it a *masculine smoke*. But even then a Gallaher International manager said that in his view, sponsorship was 'like standing under a shower tearing up wads of £10 notes… '.

But if Gallahers are doing it, why weren't *we* doing it? was the only question. Mark McCormack's IMG organization was by now the biggest sponsorship broker in the world, and McCormack clearly knew what was happening. He had a stable of famous faces and names, sporting and entertainment personalities, and a mass of client companies with products to push and events to finance and most of all, everyone wanted *to be seen around*, because it was good for your personality status and it was good (probably) for your product and it was almost certainly good for your event which needed to pull in the paying crowds. So IMG did the deal and got a celebrity to wield the client's golf clubs on TV or turn up at the other client's Big Event in a car provided by yet another client. And if you ran a business with, shall we say, a faint smell of sulphur coming off it – fags, or petrol, or booze, or anything to do with money – then sponsoring a clean, wholesome thing involving music or healthy young people with ball skills, was (almost definitely) a great way to remove the taint. 'Social hygiene' they called it in the trade. And it wasn't regulated like advertising.

This way led straight to the Beazer Homes Southern Division Football League, the Johnson's Wax New Shakespeare Company, the Mobil Concert Season at Greenwich, the MI Group *Aida* at Earl's Court in 1988. It led to a sudden and startling growth in the acreage of stripey hospitality tents at Wimbledon and the Henley Regatta. It led to armies of smiling sub-Sloane blonde girls in jolly corporate-colour uniforms, hanging around just about every conceivable reasonably up-market social/artistic/sporting encounter, with sheaves of promotional literature in their arms and an eight-hour-a-day smile clamped on their faces. And for a few drowning moments, it felt as if PR was *everything* in the modern world and everything in the modern world was PR....

Tired of the restaurant round the corner? Try taking a hundred close commercial friends down to Henley, Wimbledon or Ascot and the company will pay... corporate hospitality was a new goldmine for the caterers.

Looking The Part

Like the corporate look… As Wally Olins says in *The Wolff Olins Guide To Corporate Identity*, 'Identity will be at the heart of everything that the corporation does, says, makes, sells.' And identity means, for his firm, Wolff Olins, *what the thing looks like*. The packaging, the delivery vans, the letterheads, the sign over the door, the logo – above all, *the logo*. Now, Wolff Olins know about this kind of thing because they are one of the biggest – and certainly the best-known – of the British corporate identity consultant brotherhood. Wolff Olins have been all over: starting off in 1965 with a corporate programme for the London Borough of Camden, they've had their hands on Renault, Prudential, ICI, British Telecom – Blue Chip stuff through and through. And while Wolff Olins like to go on about how the ID look is more than just a logo and a letterhead – it has to *permeate* all aspects of the company's life, reinforcing values within and without – what they're known for are the logos, because the eighties were without a doubt, *the age of the logo*.

All the businesses paying their sponsorship consultants to get their names on the perimeters of football pitches up and down the country, had to have a *logo*. When, in 1985, British Airways got the American design firm Landor Associates to doll up their 'planes and stewardesses and ticket wallets, the logo was the thing that drove everyone mad. All the BA people wanted the old thirties Imperial Airways Speedbird design left on their 'planes and on their writing paper; but Landor Associates said no, you must have this drab grey around and about, the kind of grey you get on November days in Bournemouth, capped with a weird, regressive, sub-Royal logo perched on the tailplanes. And they were right. Suddenly, BA looked a bit different, almost distinguished, in a confidently muted kind of way. Strange – but it seemed to work; and it drove home the idea that *everybody needs their own logo*, as much as life and money themselves.

And pretty soon, little graphic design companies started turning out little graphicky, gimmicky letterheads and business cards and promotional biros for just about any business that was in business. Chartered accountants and firms of surveyors, who up to that point would have merely put the name of the outfit at the top of the page in honest Times Roman, found themselves tinkering with little dots and blobs and streaks and funny, disjointed typefaces, as if their letters to clients were never going to impact unless they looked like a page of Neville Brody.

Selling Brains

The Voodoo Arts were unstoppable. Along with the rise and rise of advertising, PR, sponsorship, corporate IDs, the logo – all the extravert, lapel-grabbing Voodoo Arts – you had these additional hotbeds of *intellection*, in the form of market researchers and management consultants. By the second half of the eighties, market research was turning over roughly £250 million a year, much of it in the hands of huge figure-factory concerns like AGB and AC Nielsen – the telephone questionnaire, clipboard-on-a-street-corner specialists, who took in reams of hard information about people and churned it back out at their clients.

At the same time, there was a growing part of the business which took care of the *qualitative* side, as opposed to the *quantitative* side. In other words, they did in-depth interviews and studies – never mind the width, feel the quality – insinuating themselves into the feelings and aspirations of lifestyle groups, rather than just doing the numbers somewhere. And before long, all kinds of businesses, Blue Chip outfits and little hole-in-the-walls, started looking round and concluding that if Coca-Cola and the NatWest were doing qualitative stuff, then *everyone* should be doing qualitative stuff. Consequently, the Voodoo Arts suppliers and specialists were busier than ever....

Then it started to get a bit silly, as the qualitative researchers found themselves crossing paths with the management consultants, who were being drafted into British business in increasingly large numbers, and everyone was picking over the same problems – the management consultants (part of a global business worth $100 000 million by 1986) roared in, bearing names such as McKinsey & Bain & Co, Coopers & Lybrand and Arthur Andersen like banners of war, took a long, hard, unsympathetically rigorous look at whatever British business was up to, thought fiercely for a while, made a bookload of recommendations and trousered the cheque. While the soft-skilled qualitative people were being ushered in through the next door by managements too apprehensive of the consultants' latest tough recommendations to put them into practice in one mighty go and wondering exactly how the workforce were going to buy into the consultants' bracing new vision. Could the human agenda do with a little research-cum-employee-relations stuff just to ease the process along...?

Then: when senior management at last grasped the nettle and knew what had to be done, they'd hire one of the new-style corporate communications specialists to do something like a roadshow, selling the corporate changes to the staff up and down the country. In the space of a few years, it all went from meetings in stuffy rooms with maybe an overhead projector and a flip-chart at most, to circuses – media freak-outs, with huge, full-colour back-projections, dry ice, coloured lights, weighty, heavily-designed information packs, young men with radio mikes, *selling the company's ideas to itself….*

Blitz Goes Mainstream

It was all getting a bit… yes, *American*, really: this proliferation of brains and skills, Voodoo Artists toiling away in anything from a multi-storey power block round the back of London's Euston Road to a front room somewhere in Twickenham. It was deeply unfamiliar – at first, anyway – and deeply unlike the familiar buttoned-down, radical-resistant British way. This growing emphasis on *communications* and *presentation* and *image* and *corporate consultancy* and *in-depth research and marketing* – it seemed to have come out of a clear blue sky and crash-landed on that part of the British economy which had to pay for it all, like a kind of benign but fabulously expensive space ship. And yet it was something we obviously did well; and it was American in the sense that both the British and American economies seemed to be evolving into that kind of organism in which the manufacturers and exporters decline, to be replaced by magic, allegedly wealth-creating, businesses that seemed marginal and parasitic to the unsophisticated eye and looked like a whole circuit of people who took in each other's washing. It all seemed to be done by the same few people.

Happy days for London, which was home to most of the Voodoo Artists at the time. Covent Garden and Soho had a monopoly on these lively new trades, what with the Zanzibar and then the Groucho Club, and all the nice little restaurants starting up. What it was, of course, was the grown-up version of the tiny world of the Blitz posers, back in 1980. The designers and media activists and copywriters and party people had drifted off, once Blitz had gone into the history books, and were working the real design, advertising, promotional world, for all they were worth. And the effect it had on the world the rest of us knew, was increasingly strange.

HMG – Client

Remember privatization? Remember Sid and the British Gas ads in late 1986? What was so amazing about the Tell Sid campaign wasn't its shameless populism or its relentlessness (although it was all of these things, hundreds of times over), it was the fact that the government was paying for it: Her Britannic Majesty's Government was doling out a budget of of £26 million to an ad agency (Young & Rubicam, as it happened) to sell a nationalized industry (compare that, incidentally, with the £9 million a year advertising budget for a big brand like Ariel detergent). Of course, we'd got so used to it by then that we barely noticed the extraordinary quality of it all. We just sat back and were enthralled by the blatancy of the campaign. But British Gas, the second biggest sell-off – after BP – marked a key passage in the relationship between government and publicity.

Privatization is, of course, part of the natural order these days (it is the water you drink). But in the mid-eighties, there was real concern about the way that privatization revenues were being used to fiddle the government's accounts (the government claimed that they were *reducing* the PSBR when in fact they were merely *financing* it, a tax, in fact); and there was a lot of friction over the fact that HMG was selling something which taxpayers had not only already bought (through the agency of HMG) but invested heavily in.

So, the campaigns had to create an atmosphere of such intense cupidity

BA, BAA, BT, Jaguar, British Gas… a new language of advertising, half 'Happy Breed', half Spielberg. Shares for everyone, especially Sid.

that anyone caught beefing about the rightness and wrongness of the process would look like a killjoy, a whinger. And the sums of money spent to make sure this happened were staggering. Between 1984 and 1987, the government spent over £100 million on advertising and promoting the privatizations. But then they *had to*: privatization was so important, so crucial, politically and economically, it *had* to succeed.

On the one hand, there was the ad campaign itself, telling everyone what a great company it was that was coming up for grabs and how everyone ought to have a piece of it (so what if they – arguably – already did? That's entertainment); on the other hand, there was all the PR and doctoring and massage and media manipulation which built on the basic premise of the advertising in order to create, as one of the chief PR advisers put it, 'a perception of scarcity' for the issue.

Get it before it's too late – and when, for instance, a platoon of Royal Marines went abseiling down the side of BP's 32-storey headquarters in London tearing an enormous piece of cloth away from the enormous share price numbers underneath and everyone cheered their brains out at the spectacle, you knew that this time you were going to have a flutter. This time you weren't going to be left out, even though, with wounding significance, one of the Marines got stuck on his ropes and shackles and PR gimmicks about half-way down; shortly after which, the Stock Market collapsed, the BP issue was nearly called off and the part-paid shares – which cost 120p – started trading at a mere 86p.

That privatization, they said, ended up costing £100 per applicant, since most of the would-be BP shareholders threw their application forms straight in the bin and only a few thousand were mad or visionary enough to press on and buy the shares. And £100 a head is not what you would call a tight promotional budget.

Still: these things happen. And it didn't alter the government's thinking one jot – just remember that for every BP failure, there were ten glittering successes! Why, when BA went off to market in February 1987, the issue was 35 times oversubscribed. It was worth £10 million of anybody's advertising budget, including the taxpayer's.

In fact, no other government had ever been so crazy about promotions, or 'communication' as they usually called it. The Thatcher Conservatives spent money promoting *everything*. Government outlay on advertising went from £22 million in 1985-86, to over £100 million in 1987-88. In that one year, they advertised the British Airways flotation; they advertised the British Airports Authority flotation; they advertised the BP flotation; they advertised the Rolls-Royce flotation; they advertised Action For Jobs (£7 million), the YTS programme (£6 million) and the Job Training Scheme (£7 million); they advertised the terrors of AIDS (another £7 million); and they boosted a mass of employment, health, and any other *ad hoc* schemes they felt like boosting, in between peddling the really big stuff.

This new arm of government became so significant that it even aroused internal criticism when, in 1988, the Chief Secretary to the Treasury – John Major, as was – wrote a letter to Lord Young, head of the DTI, querying the millions he'd spent on his Enterprise Initiative scheme and his Action for Cities campaign.

The Enterprise Initiative was one of the most fascinating central government initiatives ever. Wolff Olins, the corporate identity specialists were heavily involved reshaping the drab collectivist Department of Trade and Industry into the go-for-it, modern, logo-conscious DTi, complete with a self-aware, post-modern, retro-look, Flash Gordon-style *zoosh* symbol angling upwards from the Department's new hieroglyph at 45 entrepreneurial degrees. Lord Young, a former solicitor with a record of some success in the property business, and bent on a mission of creating entrepreneurial role models, proved absolutely sold on the value of professional presentation and on the dynamic sound of the Enterprise Initiative. His critics saw it as about as rational as the £161 141 the Department had spent on a promotional breakfast for 13 500 people to support the Action for Jobs campaign.

Mrs Thatcher herself, and key supporters, like Young, were convinced of the value of communication skills, both for short-term 'revenue enhancement' and, more importantly, for long term social engineering. There was a moment of doubt when the advertising agency handling the controversial AIDS account was dropped after two years' work. The agency – TBWA – had given us the 'Exploding Mountain' TV ad and the 'Iceberg' TV ad, neither of which appeared to have told viewers or terrified them enough; nor, for that matter, did TBWA's 'Don't Die Of Ingnorance' slogan. But there were no hard feelings. And anyway, the agency had made millions in fees by that time, and it was generally agreed that someone else ought to get a slice of the budget. So the hiccup passed and the deliriously expensive campaigning went on.

But the AIDS campaign did make you stop and think. Not so much about AIDS, maybe, but about the way the government seemed so taken with the notion of re-defining, re-naming and re-packaging issues. Just how important is mass communication in tackling the cause of AIDS? What exactly is the role of a retro Flash Gordon *zoosh* when you're trying to rebuild a country's small business infrastructure? What are the benefits to the long-term jobless from a design initiative involving re-badging your dole centres in happy yellow and putting a kind of German expressionist, shadow-laden, half-opened door of destiny on the promo leaflets?

Kinnock, The Movie

Real things became matters of presentation and the Voodoo Arts were now getting seriously mixed up with the business – the whole *idea* – of government. This was

INTERVIEW

LORD KING

President of British Airways

Q What was your brief from the government when you took over as Chairman of BA?

A My brief was very simple and direct. It was to organize the company in such a way that it could be sold to the investing public rather than continue as a State-owned industry. To which Margaret Thatcher added, 'Now John, there's no money.' So that's where we started.

Q What did you make of the place when you got there?

A Well, what did I make of it? Well, it was like any other nationalized industry. There were a lot of overheads. And it was a little bit lost in what it was supposed to do... as with State industries, it accumulated a whole number of different manufacturing processes and other things that it didn't really need. So what one had to do was to say, what is this business about? Well, this business is about selling quality service to people who wish to travel.

Q At what point did the whole question of marketing and advertising and promotion start to feature in your strategy for that business?

A It was very early on. I joined the board in December 1980 and became the Chairman, I think, in January 1981 and it wasn't an industry that I knew anything about, so I had to see what I thought should be done. The morale was low. I thought that I should see how the image of the company could be changed. The advertising people were excellent, but it was, I thought, shop-worn. So we needed to change that and I said to a friend of mine – an art dealer actually - 'I have to do something about the advertising and it doesn't excite me, it doesn't make me not want to fly some other airline, and I'd like to get a message over, but not so much to potential customers as to the staff. That's where the advertising should be aimed...' And he said, 'You should meet the Saatchi brothers...' I'd never heard the name before. It was arranged. And I had dinner with Maurice and Charles, and I said what we need to do is to inspire the staff. We've got to tell them we are good. And they said, 'Let's call it the "world's favourite airline". Pride. That's what we found. And we found it, in point of fact, when the Manhattan advertisement was run. And today that advertisement is in the Museum of Modern Art in New York.

Q How did you make sure the staff watched it? Did you organize it so that they could watch it?

A We said that they were invited to watch it with us. I sent all staff a personal invitation with details of when the ad – Manhattan – was to be broadcast. It was all about looking up. The fellow on the motorbike whose reflection you could see in the puddle, He looked up. The lady bringing the milk in off the step, she looked up. The message was look up... And it went over very well.

when the political process really fused with the principle question – not, how will it go down? – but, what can we make it look like? The politics and the look were now part of a seamless whole. And from this time on, every serious party had to invent some kind of visual shorthand – a flaming blue Olympic torch; a red rose – to tag onto its advertising. Every party had to have its own *logo*.

You could see how far this process had gone, in the Labour Party's election campaign for 1987 – in fact it was clear that the Voodoo had really infected the body politic, precisely because it was the Labour Party which was then showing the most advanced symptoms. After it had all gone wrong in 1979 and 1983, Labour modernizers believed that the only way they were going to get even with the Tories was by developing the new skills and getting a real TV campaign. Just like America, just like those incredible political commercials (paid for by the Friends of Dershowitz) you sometimes saw when you were out there, oozing through the cable – long, appalling minutes of Vaselined lenses and motes of sunlight dancing through the trees and some voice, some gravy-dark actor's voice, saying, 'There's a bright new to-morrow on June sixteenth: vote Dershowitz… '.

And the the Labour Party (the *Labour Party* – can this *really* be happening…?) took it all on board. Enormously so: the Tories looked unbeatable then and Walworth Road believed voodoo was the secret. This was a period of serious experiment, provided it didn't kill them financially. So, while the Tories were persuading Andrew Lloyd Webber to write them their Elgar Lite theme music, Labour got Hugh Hudson, director of *Chariots Of Fire*, the Oscar-winner, the soft-focus Svengali, to put Neil Kinnock in the can. This meant pictures of Neil and his charming wife and his stirringly humble Welsh background and his snatches of fiery, semi-Bevan oratory and a mass of fans and admirers saying what a great human being he was – but apparently never mentioning the general election, let alone the rather basic garment of Labour Party policy – before finally drifting to a blissed-out halt with just a still of Parliament and Kinnock on the screen.

Astonishing! We all knew that politicians were celebrities in the simple sense of being *well-known* – but not in the star sense of just *being*. Yet, here was the Leader of the Opposition being treated, passionately and utterly without irony, as a star. And it seemed to work… What was *happening* here? Where was the line between reality and promotion? If the Labour Party, the quintessence of non-presentation, was now fiddling with these nightmare processes, using a kind of American kitsch meets the World of Clement Atlee, where would it end?

The Stars Turn Out

But then, Mrs Thatcher had gone a long way down that road already: the only surprising thing was to see it happen so completely to a former Left-winger. Mrs T. was by now well-known for being two things simultaneously: partly an Authentic Conviction Politician; and partly a product of the PR Factory – the political equivalent of a between-the-wars Hollywood starlet, post-makeover. She even had a famous guru, called Gordon Reece. Reece got a lot of coverage in the early eighties, with various reports of him fluffing Thatcher up in the TV studios and telling her about how and when to use *that* voice, the vibrant, artificially-deepened one. He was also – spuriously – credited with the Golden Helmet of Britannia hair-do that she started sporting after the early years, plus the firm-but-fair clothes she usually wore. The fact is that he was less a total designer and more a co-ordinator: but the beauty of it was that Thatcher could not only be *seen* to be re-making/re-modelling, but that someone could identify with the transformation and everyone appeared to admire the *process*. It wasn't a dream: she *was* being re-invented as a star and we appeared to be willing it.

To add to the confusion, the stars themselves were *drifting into the frame* in a very presidential race kind of way. For the 1987 election, all sorts of odd names cropped up, lending their nebulous, unquantifiable support to the parties. Labour had chattering-class types like George Melly, Colin Welland and Julie Christie on one side and a bunch of itinerant musicians like Billy Bragg and Paul Weller on the other, who called themselves Red Wedge and went around utterly failing to get youth to vote for the Party of Youth.

The Tories had an even odder bunch: a terrible, downmarket, Weybridge golfer assemblage of comics and sportsmen – people like Ken Dodd, Jimmy Tarbuck, Steve Davis, Sharron Davies, Ted Rogers and Kenny Everett, plus, of course, Jeffrey Archer, the celebrity who was part of the party in a deep and indivisible way. And the Liberal/SDP Alliance had John Cleese, who made the one deeply unfunny TV appearance of his life, when he tried to plug the Alliance and their *Britain United: The Time Has Come* aspirations.

A strange business altogether – not just because it showed how far the celebrity culture practices of London's Charlotte Street and the rest of Adland had infiltrated party politics, but because there was a curious two-way reflection of values going on at the same time. It wasn't just that the stars' endorsement of the parties lent the parties added value in the voters' eyes: by endorsing the parties, the stars were clearly trying to give *themselves* some kind of Added Value, some kind of authority, some kind of *resonance*. And if you're generally held to be a shade *lightweight*, let's say, then this kind of activity might just do useful things for your positioning in a competitive world. Own up: this isn't just an outflowing of your political convictions; it's not just *altruism*. It's a *promotion*. (And what's the difference?)

Live Aid And The Feelgood Factor

Like Live Aid – one of the most memorable events of the eighties. But let's not be churlish about this: Saturday, 13 July 1985 was a wonderful day, with concerts at Wembley in London and in Philadelphia in the USA, which raised around £50 million for the starving in Africa (it was more than the official UK helpers were giving) – remember Phil Collins dashing across the Atlantic on Concorde. It was heart-warming and munificent and *much more than a gesture*. But at the same time, there were all kinds of internal – not contradictions, exactly – *counter-currents*, you could say. People smiled when the promoter, Harvey Goldsmith, dashed on stage at Wembley, right at the end, when the music had finally finished, and thanked everyone for coming and told them to drive home safely. Nothing exceptionable about that; he was the promoter, after all – except that, as someone who was there said, 'It felt like he was trying to capitalize on the success of the day. It should have been Bob and Midge up there.'

But then, well, wasn't everyone? Weren't we all trying to capitalize on Live Aid? For the performers, there was a worldwide audience of perhaps one and half billion people – incomprehensibly huge, an amazing global marketing opportunity – feeling good feelings for everyone from Status Quo to David Bowie! Neat suit! Even The Who didn't look as bad as they ought to! And what about Prince Charles and Princess Di? Didn't *they* get a cheer from the crowd! Who'd have thought there'd have been so many royalists in that young, enthusiastic crowd?

For the audience, there was an intense and lasting sensation of having bought into the charity business in a way which they'd never done before. As a rule, *giving* tends to a be quiet, even furtive affair – *just between me and my conscience, thank you.* The

Somewhere in the middle of it all – Live Aid offered another magic resolution, nice pop stars and a chance to feel good.

cheque goes in the pre-addressed envelope and disappears, or the coin goes in the box and maybe you get a paper sticker for your lapel; but it's a small transaction with a small reward. Unless you fund the wing of a hospital individually or buy a fleet of Land Rovers, charity isn't a big personal involvement.

But with Live Aid, we could give big and get a big reward – the excitement, the spectacle, the emotions, the tears, the feeling of being part of a staggering global event, organized by a young outsider. This was charity sold on the same scale as Pepsi or Toyota. It even had a proper, modern *logo*. It wasn't *meant* to be like that, but that's the way it came out. We were there, we said, later. Even if we weren't at Wembley we were there, watching it happen, wondering when/whether to call up and dish some credit card cash. We really felt as if we were *giving*. Our charity, our good fortune, was being represented back to us in the biggest, most dynamic way.

Of course: the eighties way. Self-projection, I'm a star, but I'm a caring, thoughtful star. Here I am, I'm just a regular toiler, but I'm a *caring* regular toiler, with a sense of occasion. *Look at me: I'm part of it, I'm concerned.*

Personal Projection

We were starting to sell ourselves, now, in a way we'd never even dreamt of before. We sold ourselves professionally – marketing ourselves like adman Robin Wight, with his trademark bow tie, or like Paul Keers, the first editor of the British *GQ* magazine, who wore only black and white. People became known for always, say, using a very specific shade of lipstick – 'Oh you can tell it's her: that magenta'; or Doc Martens all the time; or tweed suits – these little tics of appearance, these tiny individuations, which at another time would have been no more than personal affectations, became our own tiny *logos*.

We sold ourselves on TV – on *Blind Date* and *Wogan* and TV-am – without any sense of inhibition or modesty. In fact, we sold ourselves whether we were in front of the camera or watching from the seats. At sometime in eighties, for example, we started to whoop: whenever TV audiences were trying to sound wild and raucous and spontaneous, they'd get the nod from the floor manager and come out with these Good Ole Boy whoops, just like something from *The Cosby Show*. Studios in Teddington and Shepherd's Bush came over all Burbank, filled with people whooping, announcing to the world that they were enjoying themselves, they were OK, selling themselves as an audience – while onstage, some hack writer peddled his book to Terry Wogan and the waiting world, or a Miss Selfridge sales assistant did an I'm-just-an-amateur-but-I've-got-all-the-cheek-in-the-world tease for Cilla and the mob on *Blind Date*. We all wanted that *Hello* celebrity, that short-shelf-life, high-turnover celebrity, that US-style celebrity that the eighties were bringing to us in bulk. And we'd do our best to get it, even we were in row M of the seating arrangements.

Even the great and the good, the nobs and the toffs, who previously would have filled up the society pages whether they liked it or not – and left it at that – started to push to get into the colour mags. As often as not, this was because they were tied up with some amusing little business doing interior design or gardens or furniture or functions or hot air ballooning for corporate clients – there was a raft of little earners for the smart set, in those days – and what do you know, but they'd get themselves snapped in full colour, talking amusingly and entertainingly about the *business* in a very organized and most un-aristocratic way.

Everyone knew that publicity and profit were locked together, now, in some dynamic but obscure way. The bit they could get hold of – really – was the publicity part. If you did something that everyone saw, you could make money out of it. Eddie the Eagle Edwards did one thing, appallingly badly: he tried to ski-jump and couldn't. But millions of people saw him do it, badly, and that was enough to get the merchandising boys busy and get the promotional appearances going (personal logo? Try the specs/'tache combination) just as if he'd been Tina Turner (logo: streaked wig, leather mini) or Larry Hagman (logo: cowboy hat, shark's tooth grin).

The only drawback was that your shelf life got shorter and shorter and the publicity got more and more difficult to control. Once you got your cut of the nation's attention, you couldn't be sure how it was going to pan out. Boy George milked it brilliantly while he was Boy George; but he had to pay up when he collapsed back into sad George O'Dowd. The royals got some very good coverage at the start of the decade; by the end they were looking distinctly ropey. It was all very well to peddle yourself around *Hello*, but the more you did that, the less seriously the British were likely to take you when things went wrong. The *Sun*, which had a firmer grasp than most on what kind of Faustian bargain the celebrities were dealing with here, gave and took away again in equal measure over the years and established the golden rule – no quarter given.

All this was predicated, of course, on the frightening growth of the media itself. Rabid self-promotion depended on a critical mass of the right competing outlets. Luckily, however, there was an abundance of slots, holes, niches and spaces for your publicity object to fit into.

The New TV World

More than that, in fact: the whole landscape had changed. Not only were the newsagents' shelves groaning under the weight of magazine titles, there was a massive amount of new electronic space available. In the space of a few years, we went from three relatively staid terrestrial TV channels – broadcasts starting around lunchtime, maybe a few bearded experiences before then on BBC2, courtesy of the Open University, ending before midnight on a firm but avuncular closedown – to three terrestrial channels plus Channel 4 (1982), BBC Breakfast Time (launched by Frank Bough in 1983), TV-am (two weeks later) and SKY TV (1984). The channels started at dawn and went on late into the night. The schedules disintegrated and then hastily reassembled themselves around… whatever they could lay their hands on. *People* – give us more *people* – put them in there with Anne and Nick, *anything*, just fill the time – get something *different*: fill up those long electronic hours with little programmes, programmes for everyone, programmes for American football enthusiasts, youth programmes, travel programmes, programmes for old people, *niche* programmes, individuated, consumer-led, lifestyle programmes.

All this became the responsibility of scores of little independent TV production companies. Channel 4's output was entirely dependent on the outside producers anyway, but soon BBC and ITV had to pledge to take a quarter of their schedules from them; supposedly because the little indie producers, with their lean (or non-existent) bureaucracies, their non-existent union hierarchies and their bred-in-the-bone cost-consciousness, would deliver to the required standard for a lot less money. And before the decade was out, the land was seething with little producers – some of them quite respectable with smart offices and track records; others much more your outer suburbs front room chancers, hoping to pick up a one-off half-hour documentary about kitchen design with which to establish a viable showreel.

The little indie producers made something very clear: they were *commercial. They wanted the money.* Now, for a long time, the very idea of money was a problem in the creative departments of TV companies. It didn't matter whether you were producing high tone original drama or light entertainment – money was not your concern. Money was left to someone else. All you wanted was as much of it as you could possibly get for creativity and high production standards. But the new producers weren't like that. Instead, they talked like marketing people. They talked with respect about budgets and bottom lines and *delivering* audiences. They talked TV *business*, in a strange hybridisation of marketing, accountancy and what they hoped would look like artistic flair. In fact, they talked very much like the Voodoo Arts people, the media and marketing specialists. They seemed to share the same sorts of preoccupations – we're in this to create something good and of value, but it also has to *pay up*. Suddenly, the gap between the Voodoo Artists and the media that the Voodoo Artists exploited, was a lot smaller. Everyone was in some sort of media biz, in fact, trying to get airtime and coverage and above all, money to fund the next stage of the process, whatever that turned out to be. The days of sponsorship for individual ITV programmes (as opposed to the generic sponsorship of the channel through adverts) were not far off.

The medium expands: in the decade which saw the *Sunday Times* triple in size, the *Daily Mail* launch two new colour magazines, and countless new publications hit the street, the main question in the minds of most newsagents was where to fit the extra shelving.

Media Goes Marketing-Speak

You could even see it in the old print media – especially the national papers, who took advantage of the new electronics plus Eddy Shah's punch-up with the print unions and moved right out of Fleet Street, into all sorts of splendid new homes. Overnight, virtually, the whole smelly, raincoated, *seedy* life of the Street (ink, broken typewriters, fags, El Vino's, frosted glass in office doors and torn lino on the floor) disappeared, to be replaced by the new print centre at Wapping, or the new *Observer* Marco Polo post-modern edifice, or – best of all – the new home of the *Daily Mail,* round the back of Barker's of Kensington.

The *Mail's* hymn to the new age of media has a multi-storey atrium of unbelievable proportions, a vast waterfall (sheeting down something like Purbeck Marble, or maybe even Obsidian) and a general sense of scale and possibility, unseen since the *Express* built the old Black Lubyanka in the Street. Behind plate glass, thousands of *Mail* employees tap away at terminals in clean, air-conditioned offices, which could equally house bond analysts or life insurance salesmen. And like everyone else in medialand, they're in the business of promoting, of filling the pages less and less with news and more and more with the kind of material that has some sort of celebrity/consumer/soft lifestyle, vaguely advertorial mood to it. And so the Voodoo Arts spread like lianas through the jungle….

Hello, good morning and welcome to TV-am – breakfast TV takes off with a mission to explain.

First Sky, then BSB, tomorrow… Taiwan.

Toy bricks, jaunty colours… and suddenly another eighteen hours of television a day.

P O S T   E I G H T I E S

So what was all that about? What *difference* did the eighties really *make*?

The Catechism   What changed? Everything.

Are we ever going back? No.

Didn't we just love it at the time? Well….

Now We Want More

If there was one thing that stuck from the eighties, it was this feeling that *we can do better*. It's strange to contemplate how, at the end of the seventies, almost every part of our lives seemed to be condemned to a state of half-done, low-rent, defective-quality living – and that at the time, *there was no way out*.

You found it in clothes you wore, the durables – lumpen TVs and washing machines, food and the cars people toiled around the streets in. It was the tale of the polyester tie: if you didn't want to blow your clothing allowance on a proper silk foulard item, back in say, 1978, your choice was absolutely prescribed (and, by the way, did you even know that the silk foulard thing *existed*? Not in the depths of an outer suburb of Nowhere, you didn't). Instead, you went down to your local gents' outfitters or your branch of Hepworth's or M & S and you fingered through a rack of bristling polyester items that had that extraordinary weird, lifeless rigidity when you put them round your neck. There you go: it was all we knew at the time and we put up with it.

Now – all these years later – we've been through Next and Tie Rack and the City stockbroker's guide to smart dressing (*circa* 1986) and the choice of real ties, real silk jobs, the kind that don't burn when you jam a lighted cigar against them, is immense, endless. There are more of them and they're better. And we know that it doesn't have to stop there. We now have power, because we choose to buy. We know that, somewhere, there is an even better tie than a nice silk foulard number, and when we find out what it is, we'll make damn sure we can get hold of one.

Which springs directly from the consumer rage of the last decade. Unlike, say, the HP boom of the 1950s, this one was bigger, more dynamic and more complicated than anything that had gone on since the Second World War. A heady mix this time, a real stew, in fact: we had a wagonload of money, courtesy of all kinds of borrowing deregulations; we had access to a load of nice new imported products to range alongside the lumpy, homemade commodities we'd grown up with (we never had *that* a generation earlier: a BMW in the 1950s meant a bubble car); and we had the shameless complicity of the colour magazines which, together with some clever and persistent advertising campaigns, *tutored* Britons in ways to become a good consumer.

Amazingly, the British started to act a little bit the way middle-class Americans have always acted. We started to get amazingly *fussy* about choice, service, consumer satisfaction – all that highly strung Big City US stuff which was so alien twenty years before. You don't *have* non-carbonated Belgian spring water, cold? You don't *stock* Levi 501's? You can't *get* my Miele dishwasher before November? *Then I'll go somewhere which can* – amazing! All those years of resentment, making do, putting up with, silent fury at having to compromise on the things we loved most – all swept away in the need to have, that I-want-it-and-I-can-pay-for-it frenzy which in Britain had only ever before been the preserve of the very rich.

It seemed as if everyone could experience the new world of the Good Stuff. Now housewives in Wimpey new-builds sat around comparing designer sunglasses. Quiet office functionaries discovered new horizons of experience and taste through holidays in Phuket, Los Angeles or Mauritius. Japanese-made barbecues, bench-made British shoes, German car hi-fis – the most particular things became absolutely essential issues of well-being and happiness and status.

The house accessory of the eighties – all you needed were the palms.

There was, of course, so much free money around that the process of discrimination started to get oddly inverted. Now Brits knew what they wanted, now they knew what was the Good Stuff and what wasn't, they had to have it – *at any price.* And goodness, didn't all the little niche retail outlets and specialist service entrepreneurs take the opportunity to, ah, *broaden their margins* at the height of the delirium. Somewhere along the line, expert consumers lost control of their new consumer power and got themselves into a growing bubble of competition. The urge to improve got somehow all tangled up with the urge to let it be known quite how much you'd spent. Quality! The onward march! At any price!

But Some Of Us Didn't Get Anything

Quality goods and services… now that was the story. But as time went on… it looked like the Wonderful New World of high-style dishwashers and exquisite M&S chicken readymades wasn't penetrating all the way through. Worse than that, there were large, large areas of the country which weren't getting anything *at all.*

You could see this straight off in the early years, when the run-down parts of the big cities started to go up in smoke – Toxteth, St Paul's, Brixton – and Michael Heseltine mooched around the rubble in a concerned but nonetheless somewhat *vague* manner, while the Fire Brigade sprinkled water around and tried to knock the dents out of their helmets.

What Michael Heseltine and the rest of the government were actually peering into was that old Victorian nightmare, the Underclass. And the message was that if you really went into things, the Underclass would come out *and start eating you in the streets.* In other words – Don't do it! Don't change too fast!

That was, to some extent, the first phase. The second phase took a while longer to evolve, about as long as it took for most of us to realize that Trickledown was about as effective at spreading wealth and prosperity through society as the distribution of Maundy Money. Trickledown, this disastrous outflow from the poisoned well of Reaganomics, argued that if the rich had access to plenty of money, they would spend a lot of it and the money they spent would work its way down through the economy into the hands of the poor people, giving them jobs and the will to succeed.

Well, it didn't. The money stayed firmly with the (new) rich, who spent it mainly on enlarging the productive manufacturing economies of the Germans and the Japanese and on buying large tranches of American businesses. The money didn't trickle right down at all; instead, it kind of welled upwards, floating the uppermost reaches of

society away from the rest of us altogether, like a yacht floating off some especially irritating rocks. In the nineties, they started calling it the overclass.

Moss Side – the parts that the eighties never reached.

It was worse, maybe, in America. But it happened here, too. And it left this clear, visible rupture in society – between the people who had enough or more than enough (which was arguably a majority – just) and the people who had nothing much at all and who expressed their lack of economic muscle either actively, by rioting and robbing and mugging; or passively, by ending up wrecked and full of TB on the steps of various offices and public buildings. And while the top percentage were searching for the best of everything, this division was becoming more of – well, either an embarassment or a condemnation, depending on where you stood at the time.

... No Such Thing As Society...

The really troubling thing was that there was no agreement as to what to do about this highly visible split. If there really was an underclass, did that mean you had to *do anything about it?*

Now, this is something we are increasingly concerned with; but at the start of the eighties, it looked a lot simpler. Basically, if you were anything from indigo Right to mauve Liberal, you believed that the whole collectivist ethic had been shown up as a fraud. Collectively organized labour had given us the Winter Of Discontent. Collectivist local government had given us the GLC and a constant, fertile income of stories about hundreds of thousands of pounds being squandered on slush-fund crèche facilities. You believed that cradle-to-grave Social Welfare doubled your tax bill so that fat men in hospital orderly uniforms could sit around smoking. In fact, from this view just about, *any* large-scale collaborative venture with some sort of social element came to look like a big, ugly, inefficient, factional horror.

So one of the great, incontrovertibly *fundamental* messages that the Tories promoted all through the eighties was that of *self-reliance.* By a mixture of encouragement and coercion, you persuade/force people to take direct charge of the things that closely affect them: the ownership of their houses, their pension arrangements, their schools, their medical needs… roll back the State and make it look smart to sign on with BUPA and half-a-dozen unit trust investments for the better life to come.

The problem was that a lot of people either didn't want to do all that, or if they did want to do it, just didn't have the money or the know-how. It begged the question, what does the government think we've become all of a sudden, anyway? A nation of prosperous car franchise bosses/plastic surgeons/real estate agents, just like America, all forking out immense sums for deluxe hip operations and private universities? Real rich British people didn't all expect to live that way or have those outgoings. And the rest

TOM WOLFE

Author

Q. When did you first get the idea of *Bonfire of the Vanities*?

A. I got the original idea way back in the early seventies. I wanted to do a non fiction *Vanity Fair* about New York. And I actually went to a party that Leonard Bernstein gave for the Black Panthers, which led to a piece that I did called 'Radical Chic', with the idea that this would make a chapter in a non fiction *Vanity Fair*. Finally, in the early eighties – well this was about 1981 – I decided that I would try to do this but not in non fiction, I'd make it fiction. I'd never written a novel and I thought if I was ever going to do it, now was the time. And I was not thinking about the eighties when I wrote it. I rather arbitrarily picked what I thought was the high end of New York's life in a social sense and the low end. I wanted to show both. And I arbitrarily picked Wall Street as the high end, the South Bronx as the low end. I didn't know anything really about either one and just headed off as a reporter to find out what was there. And I blundered upon the Wall Street of the eighties.

Q. So was that the point at which you decided this isn't just a remake of *Vanity Fair*, this is the novel about the eighties?

A. Well even then I didn't say, I'm going to try to sum up the eighties – I never did say that. I was more in awe of the lives that these people were leading.

Q. When do you reckon the eighties ended, or haven't they ended?

A. It really ended about 1991. That was when people realized the money was gone. The crash of 1987 oddly enough did not dampen things immediately. It really was not until the Gulf War that people began to look around and realize that Wall Street in the eighties was finished, commercial real estate development was finished.

Q. What do you reckon is the legacy from the eighties to the nineties? What are the continuing trends?

A. The eighties became the culmination of what I think of as the great sweeping aside of standards… Rules of sexual conduct for a start, or old ideas about the hazards of divorce, or for that matter old ideas about the risk of debt. They were swept aside to an extraordinary degree in the 1980s.

Q. What was absolutely a feature of the period that you can't get back?

A. Oh, most of all I think you're not going to get back that sense of absolute confidence. The notion that you really can't live for the day because there's no penalty at the end of the line. There has not been any great moral reaction that I can see. There're just troubled souls. They don't have the money and you really cannot lose sight of the fact this was all driven by extraordinary prosperity.

just didn't bother, muddling through with private hoardings and haphazard reliance on public services. Besides which, the total private provision route wasn't that well worked

out. It wasn't *that* efficient and it didn't cover all of life's nasty little surprises. And if you were simply broke or without saleable skills or stupid or indigent or just amazingly unlucky, that kind of self-help was about as imaginable as the surface of Pluto.

And yet… it stuck: this atomist notion that the country was just a seething mass of individuals, with no ties to anything except their immediate families – with, arching way overhead, a kind of mythical patriotism to give their new values a frame to sit in. Brits were all bourgeois anarchists. They knew it in their bones. They didn't cohere in any horrible collectivity. The rhetoric about having to look out for themselves appealed – it felt right and flattering and the alternative didn't seem any more useful or effective. And when Mrs T. appeared to come out with that 'there is no such thing as society' (only individuals and their families) gag, roughly half the nation nodded sagely, while the other half shook their heads and scowled, some of them thinking at the same time how simple life could be if we really did go that way… sudden visions of a freebooting, self-actualizing world, your obligations and your expectations bundled up around you like so many cooking pots on the Great Western Trail. The Freedom To Be Yourself….

But like the Trickledown theory, anything as neat as 'there is no such thing as society', doesn't work in practice. The more the old social organizations fell apart or were picked apart (no concern of ours, now), the more media made everyone aware of someone else on the receiving end. A new dilemma post-welfare, and no real framework of ideas to fall back on.

But Then What If They Eat Us?

A contradiction: there is no such thing as society; and, society is breaking down. On top of which, we have this little teaser – what do you get when materialism meets the

Underclass meets technology? You get a world which begins to encompass everything from a thousand and one new kinds of security device on your front door, to the great imagined dystopias of films like *Mad Max*, *Escape From New York*, *Blade Runner*....

Blade Runner – the glamorous dystopia that's starting to look just like home.

We have two fears converging on one point, here. First, we have the fear of the outsiders, the people who are going to eat us: so we start an arms race in which they get the knives and guns and attitude and bits of lead piping and we get the defensive mechanisms, the full-function, infra-red, domestic intruder alarms in those buttercup-yellow-interior Edwardian fastnesses, the code-activated/ speakeasy electric door lock systems on our blocks of flats and offices, the hysterical *Alex*-cartoon car alarms, the autocameras peering out over everything from the corner greengrocer to the square-mile shopping malls. We get *wired* to protect us from the Underclass. We may eventually get moated and walled up, American-style. It's starting already.

But – second fear – we also get threatened by the technology itself. We feel threatened by the presence of all the security hardware because it reminds us what a very slender thread our consumerisms and desires and pretensions hang by (it makes you feel like Harrison Ford, struggling into his doomy *Blade Runner* apartment, the rain dripping off his coat, whenever you fight your way into your own home – *who's that lurking in the shadows?*). The technology which keeps us safe tells us how endangered we really are. And it threatens our acceptance of the Faustian trade-off – money against ease and shared assumptions. We thought it would come right, we thought we would rediscover contentment.

And we feel threatened by the way the same technology – different manifestations, but the same basic microchip stuff – seems to breed. At the start of the decade, a lot of people had videos and some people had computers at home. By the end of the decade, a lot of people had computers at home, almost everyone had a computer at work and everyone had a video. We also had microwaves, smart cars, mobile phones, in-car computers, PCs of every description – all of which had one fundamental quality in common: *they never worked all the time.* The thing you were most striving for – that car, that fabulously featured video, that bullying computer – was the summit of your aspirations, it was the thing that told you and the world what an advanced evolved life form you were. Yet it treated you like a slave. It kept throwing tantrums; it spat out its instructions; it was supposed to lead us from the dark ages to a new and hypercompetent state of being, but instead it made us realize that the future wasn't here: it was still on hold, as it always had been....

And so we needed protection from the machines! And from the Underclass! This is the new dystopia!

The two elements of the new world were getting horribly entangled, as if each was a function of the other. In fact, they were both products of the new age, part of the currency of being. Not that it was quite up to *Blade Runner* proportions, nothing like that, but there was definitely that sense of *dysfunction* if you were a hugely rewarded City broker and you were stuck on one of those terrible Charing Cross trains going in the direction of Sevenoaks, and you knew that on the one hand, your office was raging with the latest, hottest technology, that it was capable of miracles, that you could download to Tokyo from your lap, just like *that*; and that on the other hand, you were stuck in the wet gloom of Kent on a train that Ernest Bevin could have travelled on, staring out at the graffiti and broken glass and refuse and busted-up factories and lowlifers in the street lights and the general wasteland of the eighties. It didn't seem to *add up*, somehow. If things were going to look like this, on the way to becoming the future....

The American Way

They always said the Future was America. And they were right. By the time we were seriously into the eighties, it was already becoming clear that the differences between us and the Americans were disappearing in many important ways.

To state the obvious parallel, we each had idealistic self-promoters at the heads of our respective governments. They had a personable old booby who was an actor pretending to be a responsible statesman; we had a visionary harpy, who was also prepared to act the part of a responsible statesman.

We subscribed, macro-economically to pretty much the same ideas: cut taxes (at least, on the surface), get the government off enterprising people's backs, keep the credit flowing, give due prominence to the securitization of industries and services (more of a thing over here, given that Americans were already heavily securitized), tell everyone that greed is the great motor to drive us all along, have a Stock Market crash (the Americans started that one) and keep up the military budget (the military-industrial complex had a great time in the States in the eighties; less so in Britain, which was actually busy buying US hardware). As for manufacturing and all those German motor apprentices, who needs rustbelt industries? Who needs grimy old plants turning out steel/automobiles/white goods/TVs? And if you run a trade deficit, well, that's the way you run a new kind of economy. If you run a domestic budget deficit, well… that's about the only point of divergence: in the UK, we were actually running a budget *surplus*, while the US, the Great Glutton, was running a deficit on just about everything.

(Saying we became more like America is also another way of saying that Right-wing radicalism did more to change that very particular British class and value system than decades of Leftist post-war social engineering. Michael Lewis, the author of *Liar's Poker*, described how the American investment banks helped create a *new money culture* here that made other activities and other allegiances look irrelevant, Mickey Mouse, and made Britain less British. While Julie Burchill confirms how the *counter-jumpers* – herself and Margaret Thatcher prominent among them – finally made it in the eighties, when so many more of the people who seemed to be running the world really were called Gary. And, if you asked those eighties pioneers and successes who they *hated*, a surprising number of them came up with the image of a certain kind of concerned, patrician, One Nation Tory – Ian Gilmour is the stereotype. When Andrew Neil, the Paisley, grammar-school boy, who became editor of the *Sunday Times*, harped on endlessly about the upper-middle class liberal Establishment types who ran everything, you felt like pointing out that by the end of the eighties most of the commanding heights had been taken by *people just like him*.)

So it is true that more things united us than divided us. Quite apart from our thoroughly deregulated casino economies and our indifference to the art of manufacturing, we had the same near-hysterical optimism about things, the same fascination with flaunt-it, with consumables, with MBAs and business gurus, with big shoulders, with Bruce Springsteen, with *Dynasty* (sure, they loved it worldwide, but in Britain it

INTERVIEW

MICHAEL LEWIS
Author

Q Michael, how were the eighties for you?

A They treated me well. I got my first job at Salomon Brothers and I spent three years on Wall Street and then left and wrote a book about it which everybody was waiting to read. So that it went very nicely for me.

Q Now at the beginning of the eighties you were a new graduate, an arts graduate.

A I was an art history major.

Q There you were, with that set of skills, and how did you get into Wall Street?

A A very roundabout way. Through England in fact. When I graduated from Princeton I went to the London School of Economics, and I decided the world was a conspiracy of economists. That the people who were going to get ahead in my college class all studied economics… because they thought if they knew this language they could talk to the sort of people who would hire them. And in fact it turned out to be true. So I decided, well if that was the way the world was… I was going to learn my economics too. So I went and got a masters degree in economics at the London School of Economics, and when I came out of there, or as I was coming out of there, I started to talk to Wall Street firms. While I was having these conversations with the Wall Street firms I was invited by a distant cousin, who at the time was married to a German baron, to what I was given to believe was an intimate dinner at St James's Palace with the Queen Mother. It turned out to be a fund-raiser with a thousand American investment bankers, and I was seated beside the wife of the managing partner of Salomon Brothers in London and at the end of the dinner she said, 'Well you must come and work for my husband.' And that's how it happened.

Q What was the job?

A Well, it's a very good question. For six months you sat in a classroom and watched as the bosses of the firm paraded before you and told you what they did… Once you left the training class and took your job nothing you learned was very useful. There were two jobs that were available. One was trading, which was making bets in the market about the prices of stocks and bonds, and that meant taking a risk… Then there was what I did which was sales. I was a bond salesman, like Sherman McCoy in *Bonfire of the Vanities*. And the bond salesman in London anyway was working in kind of virgin territory. It was not at that point a heavily travelled region for American bond salesmen. So I was given a list of people who had money – I mean institutions – and told to call them and talk to them. My job was to get their money from them and persuade them to put it into the things we were selling. Persuading them the things we were selling were good investments. And it didn't take that long to learn how to do that. After six months I could come into the office in the morning and shuffle around a few hundred million dollars before lunch. And it seemed like just a natural sort of thing to do.

Q And what salary did you start on?

A A modest salary by Wall Street standards. The starting salary was $45 000. At the end of the first year they paid me $90 000 and at the end of the second year I was paid about $250 000. And such was the effect of this environment that I felt ever so slightly robbed, cheated. Because I had made a great deal of money for the firm and there were artificial salary caps for the first couple of years, after which you could be paid the exorbitant sums you were told you would make. It had turned out at the end of the second year I had made the firm maybe $10 000 000 that year. So I was bemoaning my fate at the age of twenty-six of being paid merely $250 000.

Q How long did you go on doing that?

A From the time I actually went on line to the time I quit was two years.

Q In the second year, with the expectation that once the cap was lifted you might go on and earn nearly a million dollars, and you left?

A And I left. The whole time I was selling bonds I was cultivating a literary career. I was writing magazine articles and thinking about writing books. And I knew that that's what I wanted to do when I went to work at Salomon Brothers.

Q If you'd written *Liar's Poker* twenty years before do you think the reaction would've been any different?

A Yes, because capitalism has become much more sure of itself in some strange way. Twenty years before there was a fear of excess because there was a fear of an alternative system. There isn't an alternative system that's viable now so the excesses are permissible. There was a brake on the markets that there isn't now and I think that brake would have been hit if the sort of things I've described were going on in the early seventies.

Q But in general how do you see the parallels between English and American society over that period?

A I view the American financial phenomenon as the great enemy of Englishness. It was an attack on the class system that makes John Major's rhetoric pale by comparison. It had more effect than anything that's been done by his government. Money values were introduced. Money became important and spoken of. The thing to be when you came out of Oxford or Cambridge was, all of a sudden, an American investment banker.

Q So, the bottom line of all this is that the eighties is still going on for the most part and it's utterly changed people's view of themselves as economic units and of their possible career paths, at least amongst the educated élite. And it's unlikely now capitalism has won that any of it's going to change.

A I can imagine an event that would cause a change, and that would be a market collapse. If we went through something like we went through in 1929. It was a market collapse that wasn't just a short term phenomenon. That might take a little bit of the bloom off Wall Street. But other than that, yes, what you say is, I think, basically right, that this whole new industry has been created that is very seductive to the brightest, most talented, young people and will continue to draw them off. And in my view misuse them.

seemed to *mean* that little bit more). Brits even started aping Americans in a way they'd never done before – instead of looking down on them as being a bunch of tasteless hicks, they started to *pose* as Americans with Tom Cruise RayBans; reversed baseball caps. They fearlessly peppered their speech with 'the bottom line' and 'no way' and *buzz words*; they discussed money, without shame; they drank American beer as if it had only just been invented; millions went to Florida; some even affected an interest in American Football. And this, one has to say, was middle-class educated life. The discovery of mass crap – it's so bad it's good – let an awful lot of people off the hookand allowed them to love what they'd affected to despise, American popular culture – Arnie could be consumed without shame by sophisticated liberal beings.

It was something to do with National Pride; it was nice to think *they* respected you again – and it was all tied up with America's fortunes on the day before yesterday, when the richest nation in the world had just got out of Korea and was about to fund a massive war in South East Asia *and* put some men on the moon.

Either way, there was a terrible undertow of nostalgia in both places (peaking in that bizarre Thatcher-as-Churchill tribute they threw in Washington) which somehow fuelled the lurch into the Living Future. In fact, the nostalgia seam made the reality of modern times all the more poignant: because, while the leaders were hectoring (or in Reagan's case, schmoozing) with tales of bright new tomorrows, it was clear on both sides of the Atlantic, that there was a price.

Like the ghettoes. It didn't matter whether these were white ghettoes in Glasgow, or black ones in Los Angeles. The fact was that the package of revivalism, self-help and complete self-indulgence was only good up to a point. It didn't have *plans* for anyone who couldn't get into it; and so we're back to the dispossessed, the Underclass… which in earlier post-war generations the British would have tried, somehow, to address. But now, in the height of the boom, we were prepared to look on it as an extra challenge, a kind of toughening exercise and, covertly, as a price that you have to pay to be young, free and strong again. Just like the Victorians ignoring their lower strata of society and the Americans two generations ago.

Nowadays, there's a lot of dithering about *what to do* – now that Britain and America have drifted apart again. Nowadays, we have a much more vinegary little choice to make – do we want to be Europeans (the polls suggest we don't) or do we still want to be Americans (millions do, quite a lot – only *they* don't want *us*)?

Don't Touch That Dial

And yet… how alike we were… us and the US… even to the amount of sheer *stuff* that came pouring through the airwaves and across the newsagents' counters back in the eighties. No, let's be honest – it wasn't *that* close: how could it be? The States had been enjoying fifty channels of cable TV for years and all we could get was Channel 4 and a whisker of MTV. But it *felt* like the great flood of information we all associated with America, it *felt* as if, after the long, painful drought of the Ministry of Media Supply years, that at last, we sad British people were finally tuning in to the world of Excessive Information.

The dam was breaking. Not only was TV starting to limber up for the New Age – US-style twenty-four-hour, multi-channel, brightly-coloured, heavily-sponsored – the press was waking up and getting both physically brighter (bigger pictures, more colour) and becoming an awful lot more *intrusive*. The *Sun* reached its apogee and went thrashing around the world like a *National Enquirer* with a serious budget.

The Royal Family (like the Tory Party) signed the Devil's Pact with Fleet Street and got all the coverage it wanted, plus an equal and opposite amount of coverage it didn't want. Pop stars blabbed their habits over two, three or four pages of 'I've-Been-To-Hell-And -Back' confessionals, or sued for malicious imputations on the printed page. And every now and then, a Tory MP would wake up to find the boys of the news and scandal departments swarming all over their front doorsteps, followed by a heap of in-depth or purely speculative analysis within the next few hours or days. How we loved it… the chance to mock our betters, the thrill of seeing the Great and the Good laid bare, the vindictive pleasure of getting a look-see *right into someone else's boudoir.…*

Even the world of radio, the Cinderella medium, started to get real. It wasn't exactly like cruising across California, surfing the radio dial as you wandered down the M4 to Cardiff, but as the decade wore on, you got incrementally more stations to listen to, more voices, more ads, more sheer *noise*. It's a reality now, a real child of the decade, that scrambled, overloaded modern life experience, with things coming at you in such profusion that everyone's a cultural critic. You have to be, or else you'd go mad.…

What's It Worth?

Of course, the more you know the less it all means. Once you get to a certain level of saturation, you start to get pretty good at knowing what's going on, who's in charge, what they're trying to do. You get pretty good at understanding the processes at work behind the stuff that comes out of the magazines or the TV or the radio. It doesn't matter if the end product is washing-up liquid or politics. If the last ten years have seen the media go into overdrive, they've also seen the punters, get a lot more sophisticated, a lot more mature in our perceptions. Housewives doing consumer group tests are a lot more knowing about product values and *image-building*. They don't sit around exactly saying 'What's the USP, here?' but they know what the difference is between what's being sold to them and the way the media men dress it up.

Now, this can go two ways. You can read it as a really *positive* thing, an example of how much *shrewder* we are at understanding what's going on and what the real value of something or someone is. We've all been through ten or fifteen years of intensive boom/bust re-education and we've been burned and we know what's worth it and what isn't. We know that there is no such thing as a fixed price and that there are no free lunches and all that. What's more, having got some perception of *quality* into our heads (the UK, like the US, being a great clearing-house for the world's tastiest products), we can tell a dud car from a good one, a bottle of wine from a case of Pepsi, a holiday from a let-down. We know what things are *worth*. We're *realists*.

The other side is that no one cares to believe what they're told any more. And why should they? For a long time in the eighties a kind of revival was taking place – belief and conviction had created an uncomfortably evangelical turn to things.

Even Tories – once the essence of leaden-footed pragmatism – even Tories of every age and background found themselves standing up for Mrs T. as if she was the embodiment of righteousness – and they did it unaffectedly and without cynicism. In fact, they're still doing it, and for her they always will. She brought people the Faith and they believed her.

But then, of course, everything went wrong. And in a completely predictable reaction, no one believes in anything. Starting at the top with our political masters and moving down all the way through media stories, advertising claims, personal boasts and the stories children tell about life in the playground, there's a defensive preparedness to be cynical, completely cynical, about everything. It happens: the royals were off and running at the start of the decade (after a good few years of lacklustre performance) with a real, class show – high-quality press fever, outstanding wedding performances, Britain on the world stage for that brief time – and then a slow, depressing decline into upper-class bad manners, scandal and dissolution. It *happens*. Privatization seemed *so* good, *so* fine and natural and healthy when it came to selling off Jaguar and the British Airports Authority and British Telecom, that it still hurts to be sceptical about it all, now that the enthusiasm's died away and the whole thing looks more like something to do with expedience and politics and less like it was *the* Shining Path. The majority regret Water, don't want Rail.

A nation of cynics says, 'Don't believe you. Tell me more.' And when they're told more that makes them more cynical. It looked as if the papers were talking about the rich and famous – the really powerful – less often. Readers never quite knew which half to believe, but after the first stories they were ready for anything; it was difficult to muster *deference* after all that.

Blame It On The *Sun*

It was an amazingly destructive period. It had to be, of course – there were so many restrictive practices to tear down, and the new Right had such a Maoist approach (revolution within the revolution). But everybody gets a little bit burned.

Hard to anticipate at the time, but if, for example, you wage war on the tired liberal intelligentsia, you end up fighting – surprise, surprise – the Church of England, which still somewhat subsrcibes to its ideas. If you lay into the Keynesian post-war consensus, you alienate The Police, of all people, who have to go around clearing up the anti-social side-effects of the big idea. If you go around spreading the word that nothing is too big to be challenged (except of course the office of prime minister) because that's the kind of radical, no-holds-barred generation you've created, then a lot of people are going to – as it were – hold you up to the light to see what you're made of. And if they don't like it, they'll be ruthless about denouncing you.

The *Sun* found its style at the start of the decade and really gave the whole period a voice. It was absolutely, perfectly, sneering, reductive and hugely energetic, it caught the readers' 'real' monologue, whatever they said. It could guarantee total exposure to anyone who wanted it badly enough; but at the same time, it could reduce a celebrity's shelf life by half. They got in the *Sun*, they got famous, they got on TV, they got savaged by the *Sun* a few weeks later (adultery, hookers, rent boys), they slumped back into. It didn't matter how exactly the stories were generated or if they always stood up. that wasn't the point. The point was to keep the turnover up and keep the big stories

INTERVIEW

ANTHONY SAMPSON
Author

Q What are your personal memories of the eighties?

A I found them disagreeable. They were a great shock to me. First of all, the extent of the Thatcher revolution, the greed that was unleashed. Secondly, the undermining of idealism and hopes, other than purely financial hopes for the future, and the lack of other standards... I thought that Thatcher was going to have a brief period to shake [things] up, which I rather welcomed in the first place: the bashing of the unions and the destruction of some of the absurd bureaucratic structures, these seemed to be very good. What I hadn't realized was that... by the end of the eighties we were going to be left with a rubble of values and principles and with much less morality.

Q When did the shock start, when did the real eighties hit you?

A I thought the late seventies prepared the way, of course, because the Labour party was clearly in confusion... but the extent of the reaction I think didn't come clear to me until I suppose 1982/83, after I had joined the new social Democrat party as one of the 100 founders and I felt something had to be done to counter the destructive element of the government then. The Falklands was a kind of caricature to my mind, not so much of the commercialism, but of the chauvinism that was being unleashed at that point, which I thought was really against the ideals of the post-war sense of responsibility.

Q What do you believe are the principal legacies from the eighties to the nineties?

A I think it took some time before the full effect of the eighties really filtered through to ordinary people or to undermining the institutions which of course had quite a lot of survival power. What we've seen in the nineties has been a continuation of the process by which so many... institutions have been eroded: the whole individualistic trend and insecurity come from that. The key change is the loss of security amongst everybody: a middle-class change as much as a working-class change. People no longer feel the inclination to work with others for long term purposes. They're much more preoccupied with their own jobs and survival and they don't have the sense of a larger group.

Q What effect do you think the eighties had on the relations between classes?

A The class structure in Britain is always reforming itself in different ways. It appears perhaps to be becoming more classless, but you usually find that some different kind of definition of class is emerging under that melting pot or whatever it may be called.

Q Were there any notable success groupings during the eighties?

A The people who benefited most, of course, were undoubtedly the people in the

City of London, in international finance, because they were latched into the tremendously expanding financial system while they were detached from local responsibilities and all the things that might hold back the businessman with a factory, for instance

Q Who were the losers in this war of money and status?

A The obvious losers were people who had no bargaining power in the international market place. And that meant not only the ordinary unskilled labourer but also the unskilled middle-class, the old type of company man, as I would call them, who didn't have anything much to give except loyalty to a company and experience inside it.

Q So what is the reckoning on the eighties? Or, to use a very popular eighties expression, what for you is the bottom line of the effect of the changes in the eighties, both internationally and in the UK?

A Of course the bottom line takes a very long time to emerge clearly: the actual industrial performance is still extremely controversial. My own belief is that the ideas that ran riot in the eighties did a great deal more damage than good. After that first period of liberation – which was I think important and necessary – very soon the destructive element became strongest. It destroyed… the sense of people working together, of long term thinking together, of seeing a world with a sense of responsibility together.

Q Isn't it ironic that as this unleashing seemed to come, for the most past internationally, Conservative parties, whose notions or at least whose manifest notions about the family, about crime, etc., would have been absolutely horrified that the social consequences of new Conservatism, ran absolutely counter to everything the Conservatives said they believed in.

A It's interesting isn't it, that you can, in the same speech hear Conservatives saying how wonderful the liberation of the economy has been, how tremendously improved the whole economic condition, while, at the same time, [they] will be deploring the whole wave of crime and the destruction of the family, and the terrible way in which the whole fabric of traditional society is being undermined – without seeing the connection between the two. Quite clearly the two are very closely connected.

coming in. The point was the tabloid esprit de corps, the excitement of the chase, the 'we can take you out' thrill of getting the really shaming details about people who were *no better than they ought to be.* This was the combination of California-size egomania colliding with the glorious need to debunk, to cut people with large egos down to size.

Does the Labour leader have a secret shrine to the man with the plan, the ultimate magic resolution, Alfred Sherman?

The only Great wholly to escape the treatment was Margaret Thatcher, whose own ego was fairly papal but who was so central to the whole iconoclastic process that she couldn't be touched. She and Sam Fox, the *Sun's* own spirit of ecstasy – irreverent, unimpressed by status, keen to take her clothes off and happy to be photographed in a tank which appeared to be running down the protesting union hacks ('run 'em down, Sam!') who surrounded Fortress Wapping in the early days.

Now, it's all more awkward. There is, after all, more to life than just *laying waste.* And it's increasingly difficult to hit your stride in government if the world's first reaction to everything is: *you're lying.* But then, how can anyone regain that lost sense of acceptance? It's much too late, now.

The End Of The Old Ways

We've never really been keen on political and economic ideologies – socialism, Keynesianism, Right-wing libertarianism – they've all tended to come and go, like the weather, modified by the English landscape and ending up muddled and tampered with and defused by the general dampening effect of the British. But not Thatcherism: now this was different, this was an ideology that extraordinarily large numbers of people bought wholesale and which, even now that the rest of the new Right-wing worldview which grew up in the mid-seventies, bloomed in the eighties and shrivelled up and died in the nineties is just *history*, still has a half-life, a much longer term of decay. Thatcherism still glows radioactively; weaker every year, but still glowing.

Of course, Thatcherism wasn't an ideology like monetarism or libertarianism or Mont Pelerinism, nothing codified and documented like that. Thatcherism was altogether a far more emotional thing, a mixture of Mrs T.'s own earth-scorching personal charisma, some think-tank ideas mixed'n'matched, and appeals to native greed and frustration. How could it fail? The appeal to the bank account, plus the Boadicea figure of Our Leader, plus a little academic window-dressing to make it all seem rather serious – radical and thought through – it was the perfect offering for the British at the time. And it took hold and spread and consumed and that was the world turned upside down, for ten years, easily….

And it was hot for much of that time. Before Thatcherism, it was daring and fun and provocative to be a radical Right kind of person, a dandy highwayman going around taunting the Liberal bourgeoisie with your refreshingly tough minded convictions, thinking the unthinkable and – more importantly – saying the unsayable. Right wing ideas were a real style point, up to the middle of the decade – by which time, unfortunately, they had become so embedded in the general political discourse that it was getting difficult to raise anybody's hackles except by advocating mass immigrant repatriation, pay-as-you-use health care, child labour and so on… Radical *was* right-wing. That's where the excitement was. It was posturing, but it was posturing with the chance of power at the end of the trail – thrilling stuff, like being a friend of the Stones in about 1964.

And yet, if Thatcherism glows on in the dark, radiating silently, the rest of the scene has just split up and faded away. Attitudes have shelf-lives and the thrill of the new Right-wing – the think-tank *scene*, boys and girls – has vanished. The new Right-Wing has become another broken-down sect which needs total repair or total replacement. The Young Conservatives have dwindled to almost nothing and the think-tanks are gathering dust. Even the Thatcher Foundation doesn't quite *stand* for anything, except, maybe, the perpetuation and grooming of an eternal myth. There've been a lot of $1000-a-plate dinners, fewer invitations to rule the world. And, just as when the broken-down, sub-command economy Labourism fell apart at the end of the seventies, it looked as if anything resembling that line of thought would never rise again, so that particular breed of excitement, that conviction merchandising, has gone for good, not least because the practical lessons have been assumed everywhere – and not least by New Labour.

But This Remains

If the ideology's gone away for ever, the buildings are here, inside and out – an awful lot of them. It was a time of *construction*, public and private, and now the money's tight again, we're left sitting in the middle of a newly-built world which we're only just getting used to.

Domestically, the Luckies have got their Smallbone kitchens and their yellow sitting-rooms and blue and white vertical stripe wallpaper in the downstairs loo… and some of us can still afford to live in these temples to the consumer passions of the age. Without a doubt, some kind of eighties *style* still clings to us, even if the Hollywood duplex appartments and Thames-side dream homes out east are looking a little trapped by the spirit of the age.

But *commercially…* as soon as we step out of our front doors, we're in an eighties landscape. On the one hand, we find that almost any old warehouse or discarded pre-war factory has been converted – either into BoHo loft-type dwellings, or more likely, into stylish new/old workspaces for electronics importers/assemblers or insurance brokers – because that is one major aspect of the eighties landscape: the hungry recycling of the past into a gleeful, useful, half-pastiche half-restoration for the present.

On the other hand, we find another, stranger landscape of commercial design. And that makes you stop and think: Where, exactly, did all these distorted vernacular new buildings come from – these petrol stations and food warehouses and insurance company office blocks? When did they start cultivating jungles of shrubs inside and outside all new public buildings? Who dreamed up that arch-headed window, or the gratuitous porthole, the D-on-its-side door moulding, the blue-painted metal glazing bar? Why do newly-built commercial buildings have belfries on the top? Where did they come from, these architectural *tics*? Had they been inhabiting the collective unconscious in some unfathomable way for years, and only the credit/property madness of the Golden Years unlocked them?

You get this sense of a new kind of scenery most vividly in the business park. What did we ever do before business parks? Where did we do business, exactly, when there weren't any business parks? The fact is that any town of any size and self-importance (however modest) will now boast a patch of land on its outskirts with ten, fifteen, maybe twenty large buildings scattered about it – and this will be its business park. And each building will have some circular windows and blue-painted metal glazing bars and jungles of shrubs outside and belfries on the roof; and even if the buidlings haven't been built yet, the local council/development corporation/regeneration quango will have (for certain) cleared a large patch of land (maybe as long ago as 1991) and built a small service road and left it there, just mud and weeds and the beginnings of a drainage system, waiting for the buildings to turn up, just like the rest of the economy is due to *turn up.*

There was *some* mod design in the eighties, naturally. The Lloyd's building was major: the luxury abbatoir, the spaceship garage – whatever you felt, it was an international landmark. And there are plenty of large office blocks covered in heat-managing reflective glass, built in new towns and the economically active parts of old towns so you can watch yourself walk humbly past in the stream of nameless humanity that isn't part of whatever great concern it is that actually lives *inside* one of those big reflective glass stumps.

But the mod buildings are somehow not *of the age*. Canary Wharf by rights ought to be a mod building, but it isn't. It's huge and blandly new in outline. Rotten Gotham revival in its details up close; it's caught spiritually between the mod canon and the real spirit of the age – Business Park Crazed Vernacular. The True Look of the times.

Terminals & Telephones & Buttons To Press

The happy face, the acceptable face of the new dystopias… If a bit of cheerful Business Park Vernacular could convince you that there was a hopeful aspect to all this, that towns and cities need not necessarily look like future shock urban wastelands, then there were also brighter technology angles. After all, who could forget those golden moments when we took charge of our first domestic answering-machine;

Once upon a time you went *into* town to work... now you go out to the park.

Left You want a new office block? You want a garden in reception.

Right Canary Wharf: the land where nightmares could come true... caught on the razor's edge between boom and disintegration, capitalism's monument and still no decent rail connections....

Above The technology boom: the computer educates, entertains... and takes over....

Left Technology also protects and imprisons....

our first full-service remote TV and video combo; our first CD player; our first mobile 'phone; our first fax machine; our first PC with a colour screen, a big memory and a sensible selection of shoot-'em-up games pre-loaded onto the hard drive?

In those first, joyfully acquistive moments, it seemed as if for once, we were really moving on. It was like a generation leap – from the the seventies, when everything was done according to pre-war principles, with thunderous typewriters, Strowger network 'phones, teak-box TV sets, everything done on a mass of transistorized circuit boards or not at all – to a complete new world, where modern technology suddenly started to look like it was always meant to look: really small and portable and black and covered in buttons; or white-boxed and silently glowing. Smart machines; soft machines.

And it seemed *democratic*. It was technology for everyman – which in a way, was the most wonderful thing about it. By and large, it was relatively cheap, available, and the kind of intelligence you needed to operate it was exactly the kind of intelligence you needed to become a QC or a history don.

It was technology that found its way into everyone's hands. It was technology for plumbers and cab drivers and store salesmen and – famously – for geeky young men who, up to that point, had never had any aptitude for anything except social dysfunction, but who suddenly found that they could love their PCs and their PCs would love them back. And of course, the fax machine helped bring down the Soviet Union because it could not be repressed. The populist technology of the eighties was a liberation for millions – it was classless and fun and when it worked right (not all of the time, admittedly) it was wonderfully *bonding*. Ponces used lo-tech personal organizers; but real people understood faxes and video recorders, democratic hi-tech machines that you could probably understand *better* precisely because you weren't over-educated.

Now, if anything is going to *endure*, it's this. If anything has *taken root*, it's these little mobile, hand-held, Japanese-designed and Singaporean-made gadgets. Maybe more, even than the glass stumps and business park utility buildings and the homes in Clapham and the new-build BoHo lofts, these devices will last, because they've got into the tiniest cracks of life and taken root. And whereas we hate half the technology we use badly or unwillingly or which encroaches on our lives, equally we *love* the half which fits in snugly, which allows us to feel that we're extending all the possibilities open to us in this shifting, uncertain world. In other words, we'll never travel on the train again without instinctively looking around to see *who* has taken the plunge and started talking on their beloved mobile 'phone.

And At The End: Retreat

Where do we go from here? *Indoors,* seems to be the answer. If the eighties was the great decade of de-collectivization, of fragmentation into units and individuals and separate economic centres with highly individualized preferences, then we've hardly reverted, ever since the eighties ended, to being gregarious and socially cohesive. People do things by and for themselves. They drive their cars and rent their videos and do up their homes and inhabit them, as so many microcosmic, individuated little personalities. And as the world outside gets more dangerous and unwholesome, and the world inside gets more accomodating and equipped for everything, then what do we do?

We *cocoon.* That's what we do.

In fact, Britain started cocooning (© Faith Popcorn) when the eighties were at their peak, when the world was just about to burst from an excess of everything, *because it was all getting too much.* Those were the days when the enterprising worked themselves into prostration to pay for the riot of goods and services they now needed so badly; and then found that the best – the only – way to cope with the exhaustion of overwork was to take the time they had free from work and just shut themselves away, in the flat, in bed, staring at the TV, eating home-delivery pizzas, occasionally tottering out to fiddle with the CD player….

… And now we're still doing it. Not because we've been working with quite that *Messianic,* joy-through-strength ('work-till-you're-muscle-bound') zeal we had before (although if we're *are* working, it seems every bit as hard, but without the excitement or the pay-off), but because that's the way things are now. Somewhat defensive, careful to use and keep the things that we bought in the eighties (like the house, for instance), rather than use them and lose them. Conscious of the fact that this, in here, is relatively safe and quiet… and of course, home-designed and custom-built, for our own completeness and satisfaction… and surrounded by all the good technology that's still working and neatly panelled (satellite TV, by now; home cinemas with Surroundsound and wide screens), we can work off the eighties fat decade and re-group a little and put our lives on a spreadsheet and think of what needs to be done next, now that you're not getting the same class of parties… Pick a decade: but not just *any* decade.

PICTURE CREDITS

BBC Books would like to thank the following for providing photographs and for permission to reproduce copyright material. While every effort has been made to trace and acknowledge all copyright holders, we would like to apologize should there have been any errors or omissions.

Advertising Archives page 151; Arcaid pages 58–9, 82–3, 86–7, 115, 119, 163 *top*, 186–7; BBH page 51; *Blueprint* Magazine page 62; The Body Shop page 134; Jane Bown, page 11; Paul Bricknell page 43 *bottom*; Camera Press page 13; *Campaign* page 137 (Paul Tozer); Channel 4 page 163 *bottom left*; Condé Naste page 48; Derwent Valley Foods page 134; EWA pages 83 *inset*, 91, 94–5, 166 *top*, 186 *inset*; *The Face* page 38; Hulston PR pages 66–7; The Image Bank pages 110, 187 *top right*; Kobal Collection pages 107 *bottom*, 170–1; LFI pages 26–7, 30 *bottom* (Derek Ridgers); Marks & Spencer Plc page 70; Chris Moore page 43 *top*; National Magazines page 99 *left*; Network pages 34 (Homer Sykes), 90 (Laurie Sparham), 107 *top* (Homer Sykes), 127 (Christopher Pillitz), 162–3 *top* (Barry Lewis); Next PR page 59; Ogetti page 64; Rex Features pages 23, 30 *top*, 32–3 *top*, 46, 54, 75, 99 *right*, 101, 123, 146, 163 *bottom right*, 166–7, 182; Scope Features page 33 *bottom right*; Securicor page 187 *bottom right*; Phil Sheldon page 147; Frank Spooner Pictures pages 158–9; Telegraph Colour Library page 187 *left*; UPP page 15; YOU Magazine page 47.